Envisioning the Word

Other Titles in
Fortress Resources for Preaching

⁓

Preaching as Local Theology and Folk Art
Leonora Tubbs Tisdale

Preaching Liberation
James H. Harris

Preaching Doctrine
Robert G. Hughes and Robert Kysar

Preaching Mark
Bonnie Bowman Thurston

Preaching John
Robert Kysar

Preaching God's Compassion
LeRoy H. Aden and Robert G. Hughes

Envisioning the Word

*The Use of Visual Images
in Preaching*

Richard A. Jensen

Fortress Press
Minneapolis

ENVISIONING THE WORD
The Use of Visual Images in Preaching

Scripture quotations are from the New Revised Standard Version Bible, copyright © 1989 by the Division of Christian Education of the National Council of the Churches of Christ in the USA, and are used by permission.

Cover art: Untitled painting from a visual sermon at Union Seminary (1998) by Abdelilah Ennassef. Used by permission. (See page xi for more information.)
Interior art: from Icon: Visual Images for Every Sunday, copyright © 2000 Augsburg Fortress. Art by Tanja Butler. Used by permission.
CD-ROM development: Sarah Anondson

Library of Congress Cataloging-in-Publication Data

Jensen, Richard A.
 Envisioning the word : the use of visual images in preaching / Richard A. Jensen.
     p. cm. — (Fortress resources for preaching)
 Includes bibliographical references.
 ISBN 0-8006-3729-1 (pbk. : alk. paper)
 1. Preaching. 2. Homiletical illustrations. 3. Preaching—Audio-visual aids.
I. Title. II. Series.
 BV4226.J46 2005
 251'.08—dc22

                          2004030788

The paper used in this publication meets the minimum requirements of American National Standard for Information Sciences—Permanence of Paper for Printed Library Materials, ANSI Z329.48-1984.

Manufactured in the U.S.A.
09   08   07   06   05   1   2   3   4   5   6   7   8   9   10

For

THOMAS FRANKLIN O'MEARA, O.P.

Mentor, colleague, friend, companion

at the interstice of theology and culture

∼

Contents

Part II: The Visualizing Process

Preface

SERMONS WITH PICTURES? Story-oriented sermons using movie clips . . . in the sanctuary? Sermons structured around a work of art presented with PowerPoint for all to view? It's happening throughout our churches today. What shall we make of this trend (or fad)? Is the church creatively adapting itself to the communication forms of our culture, or are we selling our soul to the latest cultural idolatry? That question is the central focus of this book.

In part I, "Seeing Salvation," we will fix our gaze upon the origins of art in the life of the church, as well as the reactions of iconoclasts (those opposed to the use of artistic images in the church) in various times and places. Next, we look at prevailing views of the Enlightenment, including the philosophical dualism of spirit and matter, which preferences words (associated with spirit/divine/masculine) over images (material/human/feminine).

In this discussion of the use of images in the church, we will meet John of Damascus. He believed that a God who became incarnate in Jesus Christ was a God who could be circumscribed: you could paint a picture, carve a statue, or create an icon of an incarnate God. John of Damascus offers us a key theological rationale for the use of visual images in the church. Part I builds upon John's theological base, along with other important insights in the course of the church's life, to set forth the contention that using visual images in preaching is a legitimate form of homiletical presentation. My peers often remind me that this legitimization should apply only to "good use of visuals." My reply: the legitimization of preaching only in words ought to, similarly, require "good use of words." As preachers, we often fail on both counts!

Part II, "The Visualizing Process," is the more practical section of the book and deals with every matter on this topic that I could divine. The experts in how to use visual images in preaching do not teach at seminaries. The experts are parish pastors who have hands-on experience with the use of visual images in the homiletical act. We will, therefore, consult these new experts as our seasoned guides in moving from theory to practice.

"Open our eyes, Lord, we want to see Jesus." That line from an old song leads us into the subject of this book. The song sings of eyes and seeing. We live today in a world that stimulates our eyes and excites our sense of sight. Our culture seems intent on dazzling our eyes via television, the movies, the electric sights of our urban centers—and on our list could go. Eyes. Seeing.

The preaching of the Word of God in our churches, however, is primarily about words and hearing. Preaching is about ears, not eyes. Preaching is about hearing, not seeing. Some say we enter a different world when we enter the church. We leave our worlds so full of eyes and seeing and enter a world of ears and hearing. But that is starting to change. Modern technology makes it relatively easy to bring sermons to sight.

Accompanying this volume is a CD-ROM that I hope will further engage readers in envisioning the Word. Along with study materials and the complete text, the CD-ROM includes numerous images from the *Icon* series, arranged by liturgical seasons, to inspire and enable your visual preaching.

When we add eyes as an important sense for the total sermonic experience, we encounter one serious obstacle. Some members of our congregations are visually impaired. Such persons, precious in God's sight, are incapable or marginally capable of "seeing" our sermons. There is an analogy here to persons in our congregations who are auditorially impaired—they cannot hear our words. We have found ways to enable the deaf to "hear" our sermons, primarily through signers. We also need to find ways of enabling the visually impaired to "see" our sermons.

How can we bridge this visual divide? First, I recommend that you read the section on preaching to persons with disabilities in Christine Smith's book *Preaching Justice: Ethnic and Cultural Perspectives.*

Second, some of our parishioners with visual disabilities are only partially disabled and could see our sermon if they had a handout of the visuals to be projected. We could also consider assigning persons to sit with the visually impaired to interpret the visuals for them. One of my colleagues who is visually impaired makes the point that some weeks nothing will work for him and others. He will, finally, feel left out. We need to accept that reality even as we move ahead to prepare visual sermons.

I would like to take this opportunity to thank the pastors who completed a questionnaire I sent to them and answered my pointed questions about every aspect of the visualizing process. The names of these pastors are Beverlee Bell, David Berg, Kristen Capel, Carol Gates, Andrew Hagen, Mark Larson, Will Mowchan, Randall Olson, Timothy Stidham, and Sarah VanDeBerg. Pastor Mark Larson has been my pastor for the last several years, and it was his use of visual images in preaching that led me to the present research. Thank you, Pastor Mark, and thanks to every one of you for your cooperation in this project. I owe each one of you a huge debt of gratitude.

Thanks to Pastor Abdelilah Ennassef for permission to reproduce his untitled painting on the front cover. This work is especially appropriate because it is a remarkable example of envisioning the Word. During a worship service at Union Theological Seminary in New York, Ennassef painted this artwork as the sermon while the congregation looked on. Ennassef has called art "the oil that lubricates the engine of the divine inspiration."

The dedication of this book is to Father Thomas Franklin O'Meara, O.P. Father O'Meara was my doctoral advisor at Aquinas Institute of Theology while it was located in Dubuque, Iowa. His courses relating theology and culture were a blessing for me. When I became a teaching theologian at Wartburg Theological Seminary, also in Dubuque, we often teamed up to teach courses on the relationship of theology and culture. Tom is particularly expert on the history of art in the life of the church. I asked him to read part I of this book, and he gave a very careful reading, making many valuable suggestions, most of which I have incorporated into my manuscript. Most important for me, he gave part I his theological seal of approval. Thanks, Tom.

Introduction:
Thinking in Picture

We declare to you what was from the beginning, what we have heard, *what we have seen with our eyes*, what we have looked at and touched with our hands, concerning the word of life.
> —1 John 1:1 (italics added)

But *blessed are your eyes*, for they see, and your ears, for they hear.
> —Matthew 13:16 (italics added)

Concepts create idols; only wonder comprehends anything.
> —Gregory of Nyssa

You [his iconoclastic opponents] perhaps are more exalted and nonmaterial, and have risen above the body, so that, being nonfleshly, you can despise everything that presents itself to the sight. But since I am a human being and occupy a body, I want to deal in a bodily fashion with the things that are holy, and *I want to look at them.*
> —John of Damascus

I had so little ability for picturing things in my mind that if I did not actually see a thing I could not use my imagination, as other people do, who can make pictures to themselves and so become recollected. Of Christ as Man I could only think: however much I read about his beauty and however often I looked at pictures of Him, I could never form any picture of Him myself. I was like a person who is blind, or in the dark. . . . It was for this reason that I was so fond of pictures.
> —St. Teresa of Avila

THIS BOOK IS INTENDED to extend the argument of *Thinking in Story: Preaching in a Post-literate Age*, which I wrote over a decade ago. That book began with a description of the three eras of communication that the human race has experienced, as set forth by communication experts: (1) oral-aural culture, (2) literate culture, and (3) postliterate culture. Each era has its own needs and expectations for preaching.

Oral-aural culture was the world of the ear, according to Marshall McLuhan. Learning came through hearing, and the primary teachers were storytellers (*rhapsodes*). Training preachers in such societies would most surely have been similar to teaching the storyteller's craft. In an oral culture, preaching would likely have had the following characteristics:

- *Stitching stories together.* The basic skill to be communicated would have been the skill of stitching, linking, or yoking stories together into a patterned whole. Preaching would be primarily storytelling. A large portion of our Bible comes to us as stories stitched together.

- *Using repetition.* Storytellers would learn to repeat central elements of the sermon, because in an oral culture, hearers have only their ears to rely upon. Key points of the sermon and the main message of the sermon, therefore, need constant repetition in order to stick in people's ears. A modern example of this would be the use of repetition in African American preaching, which grew out of an oral culture.

- *Beginning with a particular story, not an abstract idea.* Surprisingly, the particular is the way to the universal. Think of the way Garrison Keillor's Lake Wobegon stories feature very particular people in a very peculiar town yet reach a universal audience of people throughout the world. Sermons for an oral-aural culture would start from the concrete and move toward the abstract.

- *Tone of conflict.* People in oral cultures lived in a very small world. They would distrust people in the next town, the next fjord, the next community. Stories told in oral communities often involved conflict and conquest of neighbors who were a menace.

- *Right-brain communication.* Stories work on the right brain. They are holistic. They create patterns, images, and imaginative thought.

- *Metaphors of participation.* John Dominic Crossan, in a book titled *In Parables*, distinguishes between metaphors of participation and metaphors of illustration. Metaphors of illustration are the typical fare of sermons based in ideas. The preacher occasionally tells a story *in order to illustrate an idea.* Once the listeners get the point, they can forget the story. In contrast, parables in the New Testament are metaphors of participation, which means you get the "point" (so to speak) only through the story. Story creates meaning; it does not illustrate meaning.

- *Thinking in story.* As Thomas Boomershine has taught us, the hermeneutic of an oral people is that they "think in story." One approaches the sermon by thinking of which stories one can tell. The goal of telling the stories is that the hearers participate in the story. If one participates in the story of the Prodigal Son, one might experience within the telling of the story the reality of being lost and being found.

Literate culture has produced a different type of preaching, the style that has dominated the last several centuries. The characteristics of preaching in a literate culture, which are innately familiar to today's preachers, are as follows:

- The sermon structure is a linear development of ideas.

- The sermon outline involves thinking through the ideas of the sermon in a spatial dimension. To understand that literate sermons are structured in space, think of the spatial balance of a good sermon outline. (Eugene Lowry, a primary thinker in the "new homiletic," has made this point and proposes an alternative: sermons should *narrate events in time.*)

- Propositions are the main points of the sermon. Ideas reign! Garrison Keillor once said that literate preachers take a biblical story, stick the story in a corner, and give a lecture on the story. He said this in answer to the question, "Why do you say that sermons are boring?"

- Sermons are analytical in nature. This grows out of the practice of an analytical approach to Scripture.

- Literate sermons involve left-brain communication.

- They use metaphors of illustration, as defined in the previous list.

- They require thinking in idea. The goal of "thinking in idea" is quite different from the goal of thinking in story. The storyteller wants you to participate in the reality of the story. The teaching pastor wants you to understand the meaning of the ideas presented in the sermon.

Although the literate style of preaching continues, our world has experienced a communication shift from a literate to a postliterate culture. In an oral culture, people communicated and learned primarily through the sense of hearing. Literate culture was based on reading and the sense of sight. (As McLuhan so eloquently and simply put it, "Western Civilization gave us an eye [to read] for an ear.") Today, in a postliterate culture, our senses are bombarded simultaneously with all kinds of oral and visual information. Think of watching television or a movie, for example. You hear. You see. Often, you see more than one thing and hear more than one thing at a time. Our senses are overloaded with information.

One of the great communication scholars was a priest named Walter Ong. In studying the effects of new communication techniques, he said that our electronic age of communication resembles the oral world of communication. Our age of electronic communication, he wrote, "is secondarily oral." In the simplest sense, this means that ears return to the communication equation. The world of print has been called by many "the silent world of print." We learn by reading in silence. Radio and TV and films, forms of electronic communication, appeal also to our ears. Sound returns to learning. This is what Ong means when he calls our world secondarily oral.

In *Thinking in Story*, I responded to this changed communication situation by offering one proposal for preaching in a postliterate age. One does not have to be a genius to figure out that the classic three-point, idea-based sermon, which communicated well to a dominantly literate audience, will not work as well with a postliterate audience. My proposal was that we go "back to the future," back to the storytelling world of oral culture to learn lessons for preaching in today's "secondarily oral" culture. The characteristics of preaching in an oral culture might help us communicate more effectively in a postliterate culture.

My experience in teaching preaching over the past decade has reinforced my opinion that "thinking in story" is a way of bridging the communication gap with today's hearers. Today, after many hours of classroom experience in this preaching art, I know much more about preaching as storytelling than I did a decade ago. The students at the Lutheran School of Theology in Chicago and at other seminaries where I have taught have, in turn, been my teachers. What I have observed has convinced me that the communication forms of our culture make our students almost natural-born storytellers. Students have preached so many incredibly good sermons that they demonstrate storytelling's potential as a form of preaching that works in our time. Reports from the laity who experience their preaching have been extremely positive. I therefore remain steadfastly convinced that thinking in story is a very effective form of preaching in our postliterate age.

But this is only one alternative. Preaching comes in three basic forms: thinking in idea, thinking in story, and the subject of this book: thinking in picture. Today's churchgoers, steeped in multimedia communications, have been trained to think and learn with their eyes and ears together.

A Visual Age

Without downplaying the value of thinking in story, the significance of visual communication has become increasingly urgent to me over the past decade. I have appreciated the views of other homileticians who have offered ideas for preaching in a postliterate age (we need all the best minds of our generation thinking about this challenge). Having reflected on their ideas and mine, I am ready to offer a second recommendation for preaching in a postliterate age: that we attend more to the visual character of our age in the preaching process. How can we make use of visualization in preaching for people who live in a strongly visual environment? That's the burden of this book, *Envisioning the Word*.

Let me begin by offering two stories. Recently, I spent time teaching preaching to Lutheran pastors in Singapore. On the storytelling level, this was an interesting challenge. These pastors, almost all of whom were of Chinese descent, had learned preaching from the West and were strongly fixed in their three-point, idea-based sermons. After about two days with them, I thought seriously that my teaching exercise in their midst might miss its mark. Finally, however, they remembered their own traditions as a people, and those traditions were passed on in stories. Storytelling is indigenous to the Chinese. At the end of my stay, one young pastor put it to me this way: "You came here all the way from the West to teach us that we don't have to be dependent on the West for our preaching tradition when we have such rich resources in our own culture."

In one of our sessions, we were talking together about the material from my book that discusses how the phonetic alphabet shapes Western thought. According to McLuhan and others, the phonetic alphabet massages us in a unique way. He writes:

> Only the phonetic alphabet makes a break between eye and ear, between semantic meaning and visual code; and thus only the phonetic writing has the power to translate us from the tribal to the civilized sphere, to give us an eye for an ear.... By the meaningless sign linked to the meaningless sound, we have built the shape and meaning of Western man [*sic*].[1]

The characters in the phonetic alphabet mean nothing. They just spell words that mean something to us. It is not so, of course, with ancient hieroglyphics or with the ideograms of the Chinese alphabet. I asked the pastors how the massage of the Chinese alphabet might shape people's thinking. At first no one said a word. One bright young pastor then said, "Our alphabet works by thinking in picture." This opens a whole new world of thought, pictorial thought. They then told me about a pastor or two they knew who actually structured a sermon around a character of the Chinese alphabet. The character, so to speak, was the pictorial outline of the sermon. For example, the Chinese character for *holy* combines pictures of a person on a horse, a mouth, and an ear. The horse-person represents authority. The holy person hears the person in authority and is faithful to him in his speaking. It would not be difficult to construct a sermon on holiness whose outline would be this hieroglyph! That's "thinking in picture" or "envisioning the word."

A second story: I have also had the privilege of teaching the students in the seminary of the Lutheran Church of Russia and Other States located in St. Petersburg, Russia. I knew when I went to Russia that I wanted to write this book on thinking in picture, and I was very much interested in the art of the Russian church, especially the icons of that tradition. I took every advantage I could to see icons of the church in museums, monasteries, and churches. I was spiritually overwhelmed with that which my eyes observed. I certainly did not expect to come home from Russia bearing witness to the spiritual experience offered to me by the historic faith of the Russian people. But that's what happened. Their icons spoke to me at a very deep level of my faith life. I am eternally grateful for the brief time I had in Russia and for the visual spiritual experience it created in my soul.

One highlight of the Russian experience was a visit to the Church of Our Savior on the Spilled Blood in St. Petersburg. The church bears this name in memoriam to Czar Alexander II, who was assassinated in March 1881. After the death of the czar, the state determined to build a church over the exact location on the sidewalk where the czar's blood had been spilled. The outside of the church is classic Russian church architecture with its many domes and colorful artwork. Inside the church, on the walls and ceilings, are over seventy-five thousand square feet of colorful mosaics. It is a staggering feast for the eye. I have no way of describing what that vision was like. I was literally staggered by what I saw. I had never seen such beautiful art on such a grand scale. It was awesome! In the Russian context, here were incredible "pictures" for the art of preaching that thinks in picture. One could preach for many years just using the mosaics in the Church of the Savior on the Blood.

Thinking in picture is, therefore, the second form of preaching I propose in response to the visual nature of our culture. Many writers today comment on this visual character of our time. In *Screening the Sacred,* we read:

> Whereas in the nineteenth century popular novels and presses held the imagination of the American public, it seems that for contemporary Americans images are replacing texts in the ability to capture the imagination and to shape worldviews. Video images, movies, MTV-like programming, television in general, video games, interactive computer technologies have captured the popular, intellectual, and religious imagination of Americans as books no longer do. Perhaps this is a comment on the postmodern context of our age: Visual images are replacing written texts as the conveyers of information and meaning.[2]

In his book about theological messages in the movies, Robert Johnston observes that we are near the beginning of a "communication revolution," in which the dominant form of communication will not rely on print, but on moving images.[3] William Dyrness, in *Visual Faith*, also weighs in on this topic. He is struck, for example, by the greatly increased number of art galleries in our world today. The visual arts are on display more than ever before in human history. He attributes this shift to the triumph of the visual in popular culture:

> The contemporary generation has been raised and nourished by images; it has an inescapably visual imagination. Regardless of whether one considers this good or bad, for this generation, aesthetics counts more than epistemology. . . . Our children and their friends . . . are often uninterested in our traditional word-centered media. Instead, they are looking for a new imaginative vision of life and reality, one they can see and feel, as well as understand.[4]

Many writers also note that the visual element in our culture parallels the rise of what is called postmodernism. Stanley Grenz, in *A Primer on Postmodernism*, characterizes postmodernism as having three central assumptions. The first is that postmodernism shatters the optimism of the modern Enlightenment world with a strong sense of pessimism about our human future. Second, the postmodern mind dethrones the human intellect as the arbiter of all truth. The emotions and intuition are understood to be equally valid paths to truth. Finally, postmodernism challenges the Enlightenment idea that knowledge is an objective reality that can be rationally known by all. In its place, the truth of reality is understood to be relative to the community in which we participate; that is, reality is subjective.

Grenz argues that filmmaking and television contribute greatly to the development of the postmodern thesis. Our newly visual world challenges the Enlightenment world of words and ideas. Filmmaking technology fits the postmodern ethos because movies give the illusion of being what they are not. Films and TV shows so effectively blur the boundaries between fiction and reality that people may justly wonder if the world they see around them is fact or fantasy. Television efficiently disseminates the postmodern mind-set throughout our society.

To the degree that television has become the "real world" in postmodern culture, preachers face a new set of challenges. As words were the coin of the Enlightenment, our preaching has been grounded in words. But identifying truth, including theological truth, with rationalism and with words may demean the visual and other arts at a time when words, in a sense, have given way to pictures. Shall preaching, too, move from its word-oriented base to an image-based phenomenon?

By reviewing the history of the church's use of words and pictures, we shall learn that the two realities need each other. Words need images to prevent an idolatry of words. Images need words to prevent an idolatry of pictures. Preachers in today's world must be both wordsmiths and image-smiths.

We really don't need experts to tell us that we live in a visual age. The evidence is overwhelming, and it ought to have an impact on our preaching. The people in our congregations have been shaped powerfully and not always helpfully by a seemingly endless source of visual images. Dyrness urges a new alliance between words and images: "Is it not possible to integrate word and image in appropriate and God-honoring ways? Can't the visual be used to add power to the verbal? Clearly, if such a thing is possible, we will need all the imaginative skill our artists can provide."[5]

I concur with Dyrness. Our teaching and preaching need a new way of integrating words and images. Clergypersons are beginning to experiment with new ways of integrating words and images in preaching. Some merely reproduce a work of art in the bulletin. Most project such art on large screens. Some use movie clips to tell one of the stories for their sermon. There are many ways for today's preachers to think in picture. There are many ways to preach in such a way that words and images complement each other. The basic thesis of this book is to urge preachers to think in picture, using complementary words and images to present a holistic sermonic experience.

This use of the word *image* might be confusing, so let me clarify which of the many possible meanings I intend in this book. In his exploration of the difference between images and words, W. J. T. Mitchell describes the word *image* as coming from a far-flung family of words that have migrated in time and space and undergone mutations in the process.[6] He creates a chart identifying five categories of meanings:

1. Graphic images: pictures, statues, designs.
2. Optical images: mirrors, projections.
3. Perpetual images: sense data, "species," appearances
4. Mental images: dreams, memories, ideas, fantasmata
5. Verbal images: metaphors, descriptions

In this book, *image* usually refers to the first category, graphic images. I also refer to optical images, specifically projections.

Objections to Images

It seems simple enough to propose complementary roles for word and image for preaching in a visual age. Still, many serious objections are raised to "thinking in picture" as one form of preaching in today's communication environment. Many of these objections come from intellectual circles in the church. At many levels in the church, there exists a strong prejudice for "the word alone." A proposal for thinking in picture must seriously respond to at least some of these objections. Part I, "Seeing Salvation," therefore is partly a response to these objections.

In arguing for an increase in the use of the arts and visual images in the church's life and worship, Jeremy Begbie acknowledges that this is a challenging task because the church has often left the arts to one side. This is certainly true of the Reformed branch of the Reformation, which has a strong iconoclastic history. The church, Begbie writes, "has typically been dazzled by a kind of intellectualism, where the mind is effectively divorced from other parts of our humanity and forced to work at a high level of abstraction with a very restricted set of tools."[7] Words, that is, have been treated as the superior way of communicating the Christian message. William Dyrness similarly observes the Christian (particularly Protestant) church's recent "troublesome history with the visual arts."[8] He contrasts that tradition with more recent innovations:

> The spaces made for worship [in most Protestant churches] were not friendly to elaborate visual elements, for they were seen as distractions from true worship, which always focused on the preached Word. . . . Things are clearly turning at the end of the new millennium. In fact, one might go so far as to speak of a revival of Christian interest in the visual arts. . . . In churches, especially fast-growing charismatic and mega churches, visual and dramatic arts are becoming a standard part of worship.[9]

Although the focus on the word over the visual is changing in the kinds of churches to which Dyrness refers, the debate is by no means over. Robert K. Johnston, seeking to enlist the church in a dialogue with movie makers, tells us that the movie became in the twentieth century the major form of storytelling! When we ask, "Who tells the stories to our children today?" we must certainly consider that movies and television are part of the answer. These media clash, however, with the Protestant Christian association of images with idolatry.

Johnston describes this argument as set out by James Packer: "For Packer, idolatry consists not only in the worship of false gods but in the true worship of the true God through the use of images. As the second commandment states, 'Thou shalt not make unto thee any grave image. . . .' Packer concludes that God communicates best through word, not symbols. . . . Word is seen as paramount over image."[10] In the early church, too, the citing of this commandment partly impeded the role of art. This commandment also became a basic argument of the iconoclasts in the eighth and ninth centuries and in the sixteenth-century Reformed Reformation.

Later in his book, Dyrness quotes Jacques Ellul as the most visible opponent of the turn to the visual in our culture: "[Ellul] argues in *The Humiliation of the Word* that this [the turn to the visual] is a potentially disastrous development in that it subordinates the word and its meaning-giving meaning loses out, for the images can demonstrate facts about the world, but they cannot give meaning."[11] Again the argument is in favor of words over images. Dyrness responds to Ellul by asking why we can't forge a new alliance between word and image that will help us meet the challenge of this generation. I agree with the implication of this question. We can rethink the relationship between word and image for preaching in our time, based at least in part on what we learn from the history of word and image in the church's history.

At the practical level, many anecdotal arguments are marshaled against the use of pictures in preaching. One person had gone to church one Sunday, and the preacher had rolled out the VCR and TV set and played someone else's sermon for the congregation. On the basis of this single incident, the person was opposed to all usage of pictures in preaching. The discussion of this vital matter needs to take place on a more serious level than this or other isolated anecdotal arguments can set forth.

The list of objections to the use of images in the task of preaching could go on, but these examples indicate the challenge that exists. These objections must be taken very seriously. For that reason, I begin by tracing the use of visual images in the church and the objections to such usage in order to try to understand the issues and to be able to press on to the future. With William Dyrness, I worry that we might lose this battle over images. Losing that battle, he suggests, "could well cost us this generation."[12] A visual generation needs to be addressed in many ways, and it certainly needs to be addressed in the visual language of our culture. The church must learn to speak the language of the culture. A generation, indeed, is at stake!

My Message

The chapters in this book are organized in two parts. Part I, "Seeing Salvation," addresses three issues related to the acceptability (and desirability) of using visual images in preaching. In chapter 1, "The Painted Word," we will track the beginnings of the use of art in the life of the Christian community. This brief history will help us reach conclusions for usage of art in the life of the church today. Chapter 2, "Iconoclastic Controversies," explores the story of the battle against the use of images in the church as those battles were waged in the Eastern church in the eighth and ninth centuries and in Europe during the sixteenth-century Reformation. Our mothers and fathers in the church have dealt very seriously with the matter of images and their use in the church. The theological arguments advanced when the iconoclasts were defeated in the eighth and ninth centuries can inform us in our struggle with this issue today. Chapter 3, "Poetry and Painting," will track a bit of the philosophical debate over the relative merits of words and images. The preference of words over images is a very old argument that takes us all the way back to Plato and Aristotle. Many objections to the use of visual images in preaching today seem to be grounded in the Platonic side of this debate, which favors "poetry over painting," words over images, so we need to be mindful of this old controversy if we are to state a case for the complementary usage of words and images in the church's life.

Part II, "The Visualizing Process," offers practical ideas. There are no experts in thinking in picture as a way of preaching. Pastors here and there are beginning to experiment with this form of preaching. If any experts exist, they are these practitioners! The chapters in part II draw on what I have learned from interviewing a good number of these experts and from the students in a "Thinking in Picture" course on preaching. Part II passes along their best advice to you on questions ranging from how to prepare a congregation for the use of visuals in preaching to the hermeneutical process of putting together a thinking-in-picture sermon.

The two parts of the book can stand alone. You may certainly start by jumping to the end for the practical wisdom. I do hope, however, that you will not neglect the very important historical and theoretical material of part I.

Get the picture?

Part I

SEEING SALVATION

The altar triptych by Lucas Cranach the elder, Church of St. Marien, Wittenberg, Germany.(Rory McEwen Collection, London, UK / Bridgeman Art Library. Used by permission.) See page 58.

1

The Painted Word

LUTHER ONCE DESCRIBED the use of visual images as "the Painted Word." In the early years of Christianity, many factors hindered these artistic expressions of the faith. Still, artistic imagery flourished as a means of faithful expression. In her helpful book *Image as Insight: Visual Understanding in Western Christianity and Secular Culture,* Margaret Miles notes that if we carefully study Western Christianity, we discover "a continuous integration of visual imagery in Christian worship and piety."[1] In this chapter, we explore the rise of the Painted Word in the church's history up until the Reformation.

Before Constantine: Instructing with Images

Rather than add to the many summaries of the history of Christian art, I will simply trace the major flow of the Christian artistic vision and investigate the related controversies. In his history of Christian art, Neil Macgregor notes that the birth of Christian art was slow:

> A specifically Christian art did not apparently emerge until over a hundred years after the Gospel texts were written, over two hundred years after the birth of Jesus Christ, and in centres—notably Rome—far away from the places in Palestine where he was born. . . . The reason for the long absence of imagery is obvious: Jesus and those who first believed in him were Jews . . . [and the sacred texts of Judaism] prohibit the making of images.[2]

Thus, at the very outset, we encounter one of the largest obstacles to the making of any kind of images in the life of the early church:

the second commandment. God tells Moses, "You shall not make for yourself an idol, whether in the form of anything that is in heaven above, or that is on the earth beneath, or that is in the water under the earth. You shall not bow down to them or worship them; for I the Lord your God am a jealous God" (Exodus 20:4–5). This commandment is referred to again and again in the church's history to oppose any use of an image of God. It was a primary referent of the iconoclasts in the eighth and ninth century in the Eastern church and of Reformed iconoclasts at the time of the Reformation.

The entire history of visual image making in the church lives in a kind of dialogue with the second commandment. Macgregor notes an evolution in this dialogue that occurred by the third century among Christians and some Jewish groups. They began "to interpret the second commandment as an interdiction of idolatry rather than a ban on all representational art."[3] Through this hermeneutical insight and other arguments, the church moved forward with its artistic invention.

According to Jane Dillenberger, the earliest Christian art was developed in house churches and the catacombs. It is difficult to gain a clear perspective on this development. Many sources claim that early Christian art developed when there were Christians of sufficient culture and wealth to hire artists. The first art in the catacombs—paintings on the walls, as well as sarcophagi for the bodies of Christians who had died—is quite sophisticated, which suggests that sponsors of the art had been Christians for many generations.[4] The house churches of John and Paul in Rome also were home to early Christian art.

This Christian art came from a double root: Jewish and Greek. Dillenberger credits the Jews for the art's "moral earnestness and spirituality" and the Greeks for its "individualism and humanism." She adds, "More specifically . . . Jewish literature provided the major source for iconography, and classical art the major source of artistic style for Christian art."[5] The Greek Christians did not feel bound to the second commandment in the same way that Jewish Christians did. The creative source of their paintings was the stories of the Old Testament, because the New Testament was not yet canonized and therefore was unavailable as a source of stories for art. Old Testament scenes were painted in analogy to New Testament stories that people knew by heart. Images of the Old Testament prophet Jonah, for example, were understood to be analogies for what God did in a similar way with Jesus Christ. God raised Jonah from the whale. God raised Jesus from the dead. Dillenberger elaborates, "These correspondences demonstrated the unity of the Old Testament with the New, and showed the events of Jesus' life as a fulfillment of God's purpose which had been working through the history of his chosen people and his chosen prophets."[6] The melding of content from the Old Testament with art forms influenced by Greek sources lasted until the fifth century.

Helen De Borchgrave tells a similar story of catacomb art. She notes that the earliest known examples of Christian art are those we have discovered in the subterranean passages in the catacombs of Rome:

> As many as six million Christians had been buried in fifty catacombs arranged in a circle around the city. . . . In those desperate times Christians needed reminders of the fundamental doctrines of their faith, especially reassurance that death was not the end. Painting was the most immediate method of passing on the message. . . . The wall-paintings in the catacombs were primitive, both in expression and execution. This was not art for art's sake, but art for inspiration and instruction—symbolism to underline Christian doctrine.[7]

It is important to note the purpose of this very early Christian art: for instruction. The art was complementary with the word. Doctrines of the faith became pictures! Not many of the early Christians could read, so pictures were a primary way of communicating the Christian faith.

Soon after this catacomb period, Gregory the Great made his famous statement, "Painting can do for the illiterate what writing does for those who read."[8] Reading salvation and seeing salvation were clearly understood to be complementary methods for receiving the faith. The eye and the ear worked together. Word and image were yoked in a sensate communication of the gospel message. The sensuousness of such visual communication would be questioned in the church. We are not surprised, however, to see that a God made flesh was a God who could be communicated through human senses.

Not only did the art of the catacombs combine with words to communicate the faith, it also was a call to prayer, a call to practice the faith. Explains Jeremy Begbie, "The catacombs bear witness that wherever Christians prayed they sought to create a visual environment that reminded them of the Kingdom of God and helped them to pray."[9]

The House Church of Dura-Europas in Syria, unearthed in 1922, is a house church that was built in 232 c.e. and destroyed in 256. The baptistry in this church was adorned with eight wall paintings, two of them representing Old Testament stories and six representing stories from the New Testament. Janet R. Walton has identified four ways in which this art supported the worship life of this short-lived Christian community:

1. Art stimulated memory.
2. Art depicted the demands of the Christian gospel.
3. Art complemented oral instruction.
4. Art stimulated a variety of senses.[10]

Notice especially Walton's third point. In the early church, new Christians embarked on a lifetime of instruction as they prepared for baptism. Walton writes, "Art provided images that complemented and expanded verbal explanations."[11] Thus, in the church's earliest period, words of instruction and visual images complemented each other. Words and images worked together to affect the life and response of the believer.

The focus of art was the life of the believer. The art was inferential, mediated, and indirect. In the words of Dyrness, "It was something only insiders would know and respond to. It was not intended—as it is today—to be a witness to outsiders. . . . The viewer was supposed to look beyond the objects to the stories and reality that lay behind them."[12] The church had been operating under persecution, so words and images of the faith cultivated the spiritual life of individual Christians. Only after the Constantinian revolution would Christians be able to express themselves in the public sphere and craft words and images for the whole world.

In its pre-Constantinian phase, the church made use of visual images in spite of many obstacles. One obstacle, just mentioned, was the persecution of Christians—the reason visual art developed secretly, in the catacombs. Another impediment to the development of the use of visual arts in the life of the churches clearly was the commandment prohibiting idols. Because of the second commandment, artistic presentations of Christ in the catacombs were not images but simply signs like the Chi Rho, the fish, sheep, vines, and so forth. A third obstacle was the sensual nature of visual art. Throughout the ancient world, a strong tradition of thought pitted the spiritual and divine world against the physical, human world. Dualism of this kind was everywhere. From a dualistic perspective, visual art belongs only to the physical, human world, so it is unfit for spiritual usage.

For similar reasons, the role of music in the early church also was protested. Richard Viladesau identifies three bases for objecting to sacred music: "(1) the pagan association of music in the ancient world; (2) the conflict between spirituality and immersion in sense experience; (3) a certain competition between musical art and the word."[13] He goes on to explain that there was a sense that real music is celestial, spiritual, and inaudible. In other words, no ears, no human senses are involved in "real" music. Even Augustine thought of music in the Platonic context, a spiritual context, as part of the struggle between spirit and flesh. The pleasures of music, Augustine asserts, can entrap the soul. Augustine wanted to be sure, says Viladesau, that music was always subordinate to the Word.

This same clash between the "spiritual" word and "sensual" art occurs through the ages. It is a paramount issue in the life of the church in every age. We, too, will have to make decisions about the proper relationship of word and image/senses in our own preaching and in our own presiding. In this dialogue, God's relationship to the creation is at stake. Can the stuff of creation (such as art and music) communicate spiritual, divine reality? Martin Luther, quoted by Viladesau, offers this emphatic answer: "Nothing could be more closely connected with the Word of God than music."[14] For Luther, even music *without words* can be holy/spiritual sound!

Another ancestor of our faith, Clement of Alexandria, stands with those who evaluate the creation positively. In De Borchgrave's history of Christian art, she describes Clement this way: "He emphasized the relevance of Greek philosophy to Christian thought, and reminded the church of its Master's delight in the beauty of the world. He argued that, if our eyes are opened by the grace of

God, we can see that everything in creation has been purified by the Incarnation."[15] Clement's point about the incarnation hallowing creation is a point that John of Damascus would later lift up in the iconoclastic controversies in the Eastern church.

After Constantine:
An Outpouring of Art

The Roman emperor Constantine converted to Christianity in the earliest years of the fourth century. At that point, Christianity became legalized—the religion of the ruler. This obviously caused a sea change in the relationship between Christians and the world in which they lived. And in this era, the use of images in Christian art and imagination first flourished.

Margaret Miles names the culture of the newly emergent church *via universalis*. The church was concerned with the whole universe! Writes Miles, "Christians were fascinated with a universal salvation for any and all. . . . Fourth-century Christians wanted to make the accessibility of their faith visually apparent in the churches that sprang up across the empire."[16] Ancient cities of the Roman Empire were changed by fourth-century church building. The world was the church's new mission field, and a fundamental part of this mission enterprise was to build churches filled with artistic expressions. The paintings on church walls told the story of salvation. As Pope Gregory said, this was a preaching of the gospel to the illiterate.

Miles describes the church-building enterprise of the fourth century as having a tremendous visual impact, especially in contrast to the previous gatherings in house churches. The massive size of the church buildings, along with the striking difference between simple exteriors and elaborate interiors, created visual drama. Miles writes:

> Churches were as lavish as they could possibly be made. . . .
> These immense churches were evidently considered capable of
> accepting and containing artistic works of an enormous range
> of styles, materials, subjects, and themes. Excitement with a
> *via universalis*, a way of salvation for all people, could not have
> been more strongly communicated than it was in the architecture, the images, and the statues of Constantinian churches.[17]

Miles goes on to maintain that it was "the evidence of our eyes" that reassured Christians and attracted an increasingly diverse multitude of people to these beautiful churches filled with art. The eye and ear together were the sense organs of mission engagement. Word and picture worked together in this great era of the church's expansion. "Fourth-century pagans-becoming-Christians were drawn to the Christian faith by its visible splendor; they were instructed by its imagery, a visual program that deliberately and skillfully included and set in a new context a broad spectrum of cultural inheritance."[18]

We might examine our programs of mission in the twenty-first century in light of this fourth-century "evidence of our eyes." Mission today would do well to herald its witness to Jesus Christ in such a holistic fashion. Appeals to the eyes are as important as appeals to the ears in such a mission enterprise.

Miles makes an interesting claim for the visualized fourth-century church. People, she claims, were very much drawn to this church by what their eyes saw. First they saw, and then they heard. This was the flow of missionary endeavor.

Yet Miles observes that the formal work of theology and the practical work of the artist in the churches sometimes were at odds with each other: "The inclusivity of fourth-century Christian architecture and art is startling when we think of it as contemporaneous with fourth-century theological debates in which insistence on verbal precision in creedal statements excluded significant numbers of Christians from the Roman church."[19] Words are given precise theological definition by the church in order to exclude those who don't believe. Images, in contrast, function so as to include people in the church. Perhaps theology and art have different functions in the life of the church. Images can carry many meanings to the eye of the beholder. Theology—the Word, as we sometimes stress it—strives for singularity of meaning. It is very important to note the differing impact of words and images.

Does this mean the two forms of communication, images and words, are incompatible? Many in the history of the church have come to this conclusion. Or must words and images live in a kind of dynamic tension with each other? Images breathe life into words. Words place limits on images. Apart from images, our words can easily turn in to shibboleths. Our words can be understood, that is, to perfectly convey the intended meaning. Can divine reality, however, be totally encapsulated in any set of words and definitions? In spite of our sometimes Protestant preening about "the word alone," I think not. We need images to give our words life. We need words to set boundaries on the plastic world of images. Our preaching can use this dynamic tension, as we will explore in chapter 3.

In the fourth century, the use of art in the churches probably began with simple altarpieces that did not exist in the early church for obvious reasons. De Borchgrave describes their use:

> Gradually an image of the saint to whom the church was dedicated was placed on the altar, either alone or venerating Christ or Mary. Small scenes illustrating the life of the saint were painted below, on the predella. Eventually these altarpieces which focused on the beginning and end of the life of Christ, became the focal point of the church. [Pictures were a visual reminder!] . . . What a solace such altarpieces must have been. The daily grind was unremitting for simple people. Death was never far away from anyone. The opportunity was there to seek shelter in the church and to pray, in the magical glow of many candles, to a gilded statue of the mother and child; to stand in the presence of God and pray for mercy, to be in awe of the great mystery of the faith.[20]

In addition, the artistic expressions of the early church were increasingly influenced by the art of other parts of the world. Emperor Constantine in 330 moved the capital of the empire to Byzantium, later named Constantinople in his honor. Frescoes and mosaics made their appearance in the tool kits of Christian artists. The subject of this art was often the transcendent Christ, not the natural Christ. There was a certain immateriality to this Christ-of-a-new-art-form. The transcendent Christ was thought to be mediated through the icons that were painted. We will further explore the subject of icons in chapter 2, which describes the iconoclastic controversy in the Eastern church. Byzantium was the seat of this iconoclasm, the source of arguments raised and edicts pronounced against the use of icons and images in the church.

The great outpouring of Christian art and church building of the fourth century came to a quick end when the so-called barbarians conquered Rome. With the end of empire, the papacy ruled in its place. And artistic expression? Dillenberger writes, "During this period . . . , it was in the churches and monasteries that the cultural heritage of the past was preserved."[21] The Bible itself was filled with images. Scribes in monasteries, who were the preservers of the Bible, "adorned their pages with decorations of all kinds, more correctly referred to as illuminations."[22] In contrast to illustrations, which display visual images of the words, explains Dillenberger, the illuminations have the purpose of beautifying the text. Although the illuminations were not instructional, as in the earlier Christian wall paintings, art and word in illuminated Bibles worked together to make a fuller impact on the human soul.

As the use of art and images developed in the early centuries in the church's life, some people contested these expressions. At times, the controversy grew very strong. During every century between the fourth and the eighth, some opposition was expressed toward the use of images, and during the eighth and ninth centuries, Jaroslav Pelican observes, "the doctrinal case against images was articulated more fully than ever before or since."[23] The next chapter will take up the subject of the eighth- and ninth-century iconoclastic controversies, as well as the iconoclastic controversies during the time of the Protestant Reformation. These controversies push the theological envelope in the discussion of the use of art and images in the church. The theological themes that emerged in these discussions have become our bedrock theological themes for the justification of the use of the "Painted Word" in the life of the church today.

As this very brief history suggests, "seeing salvation" was an important component of the life of the church. A few snapshots of the later development of art strengthen that point. For an imposing example, consider the Church of Saint-Denis, which was rebuilt completely during the leadership of Abbot Suger (1122–1151). By that time, the established church had moved far from its roots in the catacombs to a dominant, powerful place in society. Many of the churches built in this era openly display this power. Janet R. Walton describes the Church of Saint-Denis this way:

> The gothic structure of Saint-Denis attests to particular qualities of God and the divine/human relationship. It testifies to the magnificence of God, an abundance and a loftiness far beyond our ability to imagine. As a building that towered over other structures, the abbey church marked the distinctive identity of God, a source of unique power and authority. . . .

> The gothic design of Saint-Denis separated religious activity
> from the normal experience of the community. It represented
> the "otherness" of God through its size as well as its ornate-
> ness. The architectural style of the church and the theology
> that shaped the worship worked in perfect partnership. The
> mystery of God was embodied in both.[24]

According to Jane Dillenberger, gothic design in church building—a design that is still on display in America in our time—
emphasizes majesty, serenity, and lyricism. The focus of religious
life during the medieval times had shifted from the monasteries to
the cathedrals and city churches. The art in these magnificent edi-
fices was the story of salvation told in artistic form for the common
people, focusing on the earthly life of Jesus. Most ideas for these
paintings came from the Bible, and a highly beloved figure was
the person of Mary. Dillenberger describes the significance of this
artistic expression: "The art of the medieval cathedral was a great
encyclopedia of religious thought symbolized in stone. The gothic
cathedral has been called the Bible of the poor, for those who could
not read could yet see the content of the Bible in the wood and
stone carvings and in the stained glass of the cathedral windows."[25]

Medieval churches were distinguished by their emphasis of the
visual. This may be the one period in the church's history where the
visual dimension actually dominated the verbal dimension in the
communication of the faith. Eye dominated ear. Sight dominated
hearing. Image dominated word. Hear Margaret Miles again:

> The new, painted chapels and churches were in striking con-
> trast to the "stony and dark" churches of the twelfth and thir-
> teenth centuries. By the end of the fourteenth century, walls
> were covered with frescoes, and church buildings were being
> designed or modified to ensure adequate lighting of the fres-
> coes. Carved pulpits, free-standing sculpture, painted panels,
> and frescoes filled the churches. Above the high altar was hung
> a large painting and over it, suspended from the ceiling or
> vault, was usually a great crucifix.[26]

A wonderful world for the eye! This was truly "seeing salvation."

John of Genoa in his *Catholicon* speaks of the purpose of the
images that were becoming so popular in the churches:

Know that there were three reasons for the institution of images in churches. First, for the instruction of simple people, because they are instructed by them as if by books. Second, so that the mystery of the incarnation and the examples of the saints may be the more active in our memory through being presented daily to our eyes. Third, to excite feelings of devotion, these being aroused more effectively by things seen than by things heard.[27]

John gives here a real pep talk for the eye. He suggests that devotion is aroused more fully by the eye than by the ear.

What happened to preaching in such a world? Might not the feast for the eye in the very architecture of the building overwhelm attempts to offer a word for the ear? In fact, writes Miles, preaching of the period took its clue from the world of the eye:

The new vivid style of public preaching of the fourteenth century imitated the emotional intensity of religious paintings and devotional treatises. . . . Franciscan and Dominican preachers, in the course of the liturgical year, recounted and interpreted the events depicted on the walls of the church, using the gestures and postures of the painted figures. Late-medieval preachers were "skilled visual performers" who used a repertoire of gestures known to their audiences from paintings. Manuals of such gestures existed, providing a stylized body language that accompanied and heightened the verbal communication. The dramatic visual intensity of sermons sometimes even threatened to entirely overwhelm their verbal content.[28]

Here is preaching as thinking in picture. Almost the very text of the sermon is what the eyes can see in the splendor of the church itself. Thinking in picture, therefore, is not some new innovation. The historical roots of such preaching are anchored in ancient church practice. The use of visualization in preaching in the twenty-first century is well grounded in the church's life.

A comment about today's church architecture may also be in order here. As we have seen, one of the primary functions of gothic cathedrals was to enable people to "see salvation." The artwork was powerful and overwhelming. It is rather astonishing to compare the visual component of church architecture then and now. Today many new "generic" churches are rising throughout our land. In very few of these churches would one see salvation. It is somewhat strange that in our visual age, so many churches are built with so few visuals as part of the church's structure. It is doubtful that the visuals projected during a church service fulfill for the worship life of these congregations the need for seeing salvation that the church in other ages understood and created!

Eve of Reformation: Image and Word Out of Balance

We have seen how the medieval church was dominated by paintings, images, icons, and sculptures. It was a time of visual splendor in the church. Visualization permeated church life on the eve of the Reformation.

There are problems with visualization, however, when it is not boundaried by the Word. Carlos M. N. Eire, among others, points to the problems this raised for the church:

> The map of Europe bristled with holy places; life pulsated with the expectation of the miraculous. In the popular mind and in much of the official teaching of the church, almost anything was possible. . . . Late medieval religion sought to grasp the transcendent by making it immanent: It was a religion that sought to embody itself in images, reduce the infinite to the finite, blend the holy and the profane, and disintegrate all mystery.[29]

This rather dire portrayal of the problem comes from a scholar who argues for the legitimate work of iconoclasm as carried out by the "Reformed" wing of the Reformation. The goal of medieval religion in Eire's view was the zeal to tap supernatural power and thereby win a guarantee of salvation. Images and icons were understood to be the medium through which supernatural power was available to humans. Such is the theology behind this era of visual splendor.

Eire sees many problems in this visual world of faith. There were many pious frauds. The "true cross" was everywhere. The Mass became an idol. (The "Reformed" Reformation was centrally about true worship.) There was a cult of images. Superstition reigned. Such superstition is understandable. Recall that images need words to give boundaries to their meanings because people see many things in images. When image is allowed to roam free, there is certainly a possibility of superstition. Images call forth from people anything they want to think. Because images need boundaries, the dominance of the visual in this period of the church's life became problematic.

William Dyrness notes that when Martin Luther went to Rome in the early part of his life, he saw superstition and extravagance associated with images and relics. "Indeed, Luther is supposed to have said that St. Peter's itself was 'built with the flesh, skin, and bones of the flock.'"[30] Margaret Miles puts the matter this way: "An imbalance between engagement of the visual sense and of the auditory sense of the worship became a focus of both Roman Catholic and Protestant reformers. Both recognized the need to increase auditory aspects of worship and religious instruction."[31]

That's where we are on the eve of the Reformation. An imbalance in the use of the visual in relationship to the auditory had occurred over time. The visual sense dominated, but the visual sense without the sense of hearing the Word of God leads to a variety of problems. (Likewise, the auditory sense without the balance of the visual sense leads to its own set of problems.) These problems were addressed most radically by the "Reformed" branch of the Reformation.

At times when there was a sentiment that picture was dominating word, when eye was dominating ear, iconoclasm—a fight against the use of images and the visual sense—has been a primary approach of the church. Iconoclasm arose in the Eastern church in the eighth and ninth centuries, and it arose again in the time of the Reformation. We turn in the next chapter to a more detailed study of these two iconoclastic movements in the church's life. These debates are crucial to our understanding of the use of the visual sense in the life of the church. They contain all the arguments against images, against the use of the visual sense—and the best arguments favoring the use of the visual sense as well. The ideas in the next chapter therefore stand at the epicenter of the case for visualization in worship and preaching.

2

Iconoclastic Controversies

IN GENERAL, an iconoclast is someone who destroys religious images or opposes their veneration. Jeremy Begbie defines iconoclasts in terms of their goals: "'Iconoclasts'—those who rejected the use of icons and sought their destruction—argued that images of Christ, representing as they did his physical appearance, diminished his divinity by revealing only his humanity."[1] Lee Palmer Wandel defines the work of iconoclasts in terms of violence: "Iconoclasm is defined by its objects, its 'victims' and the focus of its violence. . . . 'Iconoclasm' is defined as an attack, violence, either verbal or physical, usually physical, often combined with violent words, against 'images', predominantly, but not exclusively in churches."[2]

Strong opposition to the use of images arose at key times in the life of the church. In this chapter, we will examine the iconoclastic controversies that occurred in the Eastern church in the eighth and ninth centuries and in the Reformed Reformation churches in Europe in the sixteenth century. Their concerns present an important issue for those of us who are "iconophiles" (people who love icons) seeking to encourage the use of images in the task of preaching. Clearly, if the iconoclasts are correct, the use of images for Christian preaching becomes unsupportable.

Iconoclasm in the Eastern Church

Iconoclasm in the East flowed from an edict Emperor Leo III issued in 725 C.E., ordering that icons be removed from churches and homes and be destroyed. Part of Leo's rationale may have been to prevent further spread of Islam.[3] Islam forbade and still forbids religious images, so the images used by Christians were an offense to Muslims. Banning the use of images might therefore remove a stumbling block for Muslims. Jaroslav Pelikan suggests a second, more political rationale for the prohibition of religious images: that the emperor wanted there to be no images but his own.[4]

The rulings about images went back and forth over the next 120 years. In 787 the Second Council of Nicea restored the cult of images for the life of Eastern Christianity, declaring that icons were orthodox and God-pleasing. Emperor Leo V in 813 issued a second edict banning the use of icons. With the death of Emperor Theophilus in 842, imperial objections to the use of icons came to an end. In 843 Empress Theodora convened a council that affirmed the teaching of the Seven Ecumenical Councils and confirmed the place of the icon in Christian life and worship.

Pelikan notes that the opponents of images were emperors, not empresses. That observation suggests that a disturbing pattern was emerging in Eastern thought. Empresses, in permitting images, allowed a sensual way of depicting the manifold life of the church. Hence, images were often referred to as "feminine" and earthly because the sensual world was associated with females, and the fact that empresses favored icons underscored this connection. The "masculine," in contrast, upholds the virtue of the *immaterial idea.* As ideas were pitted against images, masculine was pitted against feminine in the thought of the church. That is, the spiritual, seen as masculine, was pitted against the earthly, which is feminine. These distinctions haunt the history of the debate on the relative merit of words and ideas. Since men have been the *dominant* shapers of culture throughout history, it should not be surprising that in the history of thought, ideas have almost always been considered superior to images. I am increasingly convinced that this conflict between the relative merits of words and images (with words winning the battle) stands behind much of the contemporary objection to the use of images in preaching. This situation is discussed in chapter 3.

This conflict between divine spiritual reality and earthly corruption forms another of the objections to icons. Pelikan offers as an example the Iconoclastic Synod of 754, which criticized "'worthless and dead matter'" as "an unworthy instrument for authentic worship." Mental contemplation is, therefore, the appropriate means of worship, because "God is spirit," as Jesus says in John 4:24.[5] In opposing images on "spiritual" grounds, the iconoclasts disparaged everything about Christ that was physical and visible. This way of thinking is in marked contrast to the school of Martin Luther, in whose ways I was tutored. Luther talked about God revealing God-self "deep in the flesh" of Jesus. He gloried in matter in his christological musings.

A fourth rationale given against the use of images may be the most important reason of all. This opposition is based on the second commandment: "You shall not make for yourself an idol, whether in the form of anything that is in heaven above, or that is on the earth beneath, or that is in the water under the earth. You shall not bow down to them or worship them" (Exodus 20:4–5). We have here a strong biblical word against any form of idolatry. Idolatry is, indeed, the temptation of the eye. The Jewish and Muslim religious communities adhered to this commandment forbidding idols, as we discussed briefly in chapter 1. This commandment presented a strong challenge to the use of images in the Eastern church.

John of Damascus:
The Doctor of Christian Art

The most important theologian in championing the cause of icons was John of Damascus (676–749). He lived in a monastery southeast of Jerusalem under Islamic rule, so he was not subject to the edicts of the emperor. John wrote a book titled *On the Divine Images: Three Apologies against Those Who Attack the Divine Images.*[6] We will turn our attention first to his defense (a victorious defense, I might add) for the use of images.

Theologically, John understood the Christology of his opponents to be very close to that of Eutychus and to Manichaeism and Docetism. In John's mind, these Christologies downplayed the humanity of Jesus. This is the same sort of dualism we have discussed earlier. The ideological context of ancient Greece and everyone it influenced was a dualistic context. Spirit and matter, God and human, divine and earthly were the poles of this dualism. This dualism was the dominant philosophical force in most of the christological heresies. The dualistic mind-set simply could not conceive of Jesus as both divine and human in one person; it was a philosophical impossibility. So a host of heretical Christologies minimized the full humanity of Jesus, and those who argued for the full physical, earthly humanity of Jesus were often accused of worshiping matter. John of Damascus replied, "I do not worship matter, but I worship the creator of matter who became matter for my sake."[7]

According to John, therefore, matter can be an instrument of divinity. But he did not worship matter! David Anderson's translation of John's book distinguishes "adoration" from veneration and honor. God alone receives adoration. Humans can make images of the God whom they have seen with their own eyes in Jesus Christ, but they dare not "adore" such images. "I honor the image," writes John, "but not as God."[8]

As far as John of Damascus is concerned, the use of images for personal and corporate devotion is the church's tradition. He makes this point over and over again. The use of the visual arts goes back to the beginning of the church's life. The Bible, he says, overwhelmingly supports such a tradition. He puts the second commandment about images in the context of the whole Bible. He particularly quotes Old Testament passages that give divine directions on how to make use of art and artwork in the temple. In an argument that is directed primarily to the Jews, John simply makes the point that he is upholding the biblical tradition and the tradition of the fathers of the church: "Accept, therefore, the teaching of the Scriptures and the fathers."[9]

John of Damascus does not recoil from the materiality of the world. He revels in it. He celebrates it. Eye and ear are windows into the world of the divine as presented to us in Jesus Christ. John glories in the senses of seeing and hearing:

> We use all our senses to produce worthy images of Him, we sanctify the noblest of the senses, which is that of sight. For just as words edify the ear, so also the image stimulates the eye. What the book is to the literate, the image is to the illiterate. Just as words speak to the ear, so the image speaks to the sight; it brings us understanding.[10]

John speaks of eye and ear as equal instruments of divine presence. He holds the two in balance, although he seems to grant to the sense of sight the title of "noblest." In contrast, in the Western dichotomy that developed between words for ears and images for eyes, the senses relating to the word are almost always lifted up as superior to what we can see with our eyes. We will need to remember John of Damascus in our final formulation of the relative value of our senses in receiving divine revelation. John asserts very strongly that the eye, too, is a means of grace. Divinity can be present for humanity through our eyes. We can see salvation!

John of Damascus wants to *see* salvation. He sarcastically allows that his enemies, the iconoclasts, are superior to him in faith. As for himself, he is simply human, so he wants to see: "You perhaps, are superior to me, and have risen so far above bodily things that you have become virtually immaterial and feel free to make light of all visible things, but since I am human and clothed with a body, I desire to see and be present with the saints physically."[11]

In his Second Apology, John of Damascus makes many of the same arguments. He is constantly refuting the assertion that images are idolatrous and a violation of the second commandment. Over and over, he cites the Old Testament temple as a building that provided a good share of visual accompaniment to its worship. He argues as well that no emperor has the right to make laws for the church. He also never loses sight of the Manichaeans, who claim that since matter is evil, it cannot be used as a vehicle for divine presence. For his response to that claim, John turns to the book of Genesis, which says the creation is good. He turns this argument also upon the Jewish opposition to the use of created images. In summary at the end of the Second Apology, he writes, "Receive as a single stream the testimony of Scripture and the fathers; it shows you that the making and worship of images is no new invention, but the ancient tradition of the Church,"[12] and, "We are not inventing a new faith."[13]

In the Third Apology, John of Damascus argues again that icons are a means of Christ's presence with us. Christ continues to be revealed through our ears and through our eyes:

> Since [Christ] is no longer physically present, we hear His words and read from books and by hearing our souls are sanctified and filled with blessing, and so we worship, honoring the books from which we hear His words. So also, through the painting of images, we are able to contemplate the likeness of His bodily form, His miracles, and His passion, and thus are sanctified, blessed, and filled with joy.[14]

Note the power of the painted image. It is, indeed, a means of grace. Through the image, we are sanctified, blessed, filled with joy. This is high praise for the painted word. Through the painted word, we do see salvation.

One final quote from the Third Apology underlines John's sense of sacramental seeing. Here, John explains why images are made:

> All images reveal and make perceptible those things which are hidden. . . . The image was devised that [we] might advance in knowledge, and that secret things might be revealed and made perceptible. Therefore, images are a source of profit, help, and salvation for all, since they make things so obviously manifest, enabling us to perceive hidden things.[15]

John again describes images as active in our salvation. They are a source of profit and help. They reveal the unseen, hidden things.

These arguments by John of Damascus prevailed over the arguments of the iconoclasts. Had it not been for John, we might have a very different church today. The role of artistic expression in Christendom could have gone another way. But in the end, painted images and icons were not prohibited. Seeing salvation with one's eyes was affirmed as one of God's ways of revealing Godself to humans, thanks to this Doctor of Christian Art.

What the Bible Says

The debates over icons are vital for the church's understanding of the visual dimension of the faith. Pelikan says of these debates, "During the entire Middle Ages in the West there was never as lively a theological examination of the relations between religion and art as there was among the Greek theologians."[16] He also calls this controversy "the first thoroughgoing debate in the history of the church about the nature and function of religious art and the possibility of a Christian aesthetic."[17] These debates have much to teach us as we evaluate the visual dimension of the Christian faith in our own time.

Particularly relevant are the important biblical quotations that were part of the iconoclastic debate. As we already have discussed, one of these passages is the second commandment, which denounces idolatry. Christians in every age will need to come to terms with this commandment's implications for the visual arts. We have seen that John of Damascus juxtaposed the second commandment with other biblical divine commandments to artistically beautify the ancient temple. An example of passages related to John's argument is Exodus 35. In the following pages, we will consider other biblical passages that played a part in the debate over icons.

Simeon Sees God's Salvation

Simeon of old first sees Jesus in the temple (Luke 2:29–32). It is through his seeing with the eyes that salvation is granted to him: "'Master, now you are dismissing your servant in peace, according to your word; for my *eyes have seen your salvation . . .* a light for revelation to the Gentiles and for glory to your people Israel'" (emphasis added). In this passage, salvation is offered to Simeon through the gift of seeing.

Blessed Are Your Eyes

Within a series of parables, Jesus says to his disciples, "But blessed are *your eyes, for they see,* and your ears, for they hear. Truly I tell you, many prophets and righteous people longed to see what you see, but did not see it, and to hear what you hear, but did not hear it" (Matthew 13:16–17, emphasis added). Pelikan gives rapt attention to the use of this passage in the iconoclastic debates. His conclusions are very important for our own discussions of the sense of seeing in the church:

> When Christ said, "Blessed are your eyes . . . and ears," he gave his endorsement to the quest for beatitude through seeing, and therefore for the use of icons as a present-day substitute for the miracles and other deeds which his disciples were privileged to behold. . . . Each of the senses was hallowed by the saving action of God. Sight, as the primary sense, was hallowed through the visible appearing of God in Christ, just as hearing was hallowed through the word of God. The icon served as a means for this hallowing of sight, combined as it was with the hearing of the word. . . . When they put such an emphasis on the role of the senses in worship, the iconophiles were affirming the role of the body in salvation.[18]

Here is the very heart of the iconophiles' argument. Eyes are blessed by God. The visible appearance of God in Jesus Christ hallows the eyes. Eyes and ears, created by God, work together in our salvation. They become means of grace for us, as God comes to us through sight and sound. Eyes and ears, along with our entire body, receive the gift of salvation.

We Have Seen It with Our Eyes

The writer of 1 John assures his readers, "We declare to you what was from the beginning, what we have heard, *what we have seen with our eyes*, what we have looked at and touched with our hands, concerning the word of life—this life was revealed, and we have *seen it* and testify to it, and declare to you the eternal life that was with the Father and was revealed to us—we declare to you what we have *seen* and heard" (1 John 1:1–3, emphasis added). According to Pelikan, the iconophiles saw in this passage an argument for equality between eye and ear:

> The genuineness of the incarnation meant that these scenes and these objects were to be portrayed as "graphically" as possible, whether in words or in icons. . . . The same content was being set forth in the icons and in the accounts of the Gospels, and "the same history" was to be seen in both. . . . The iconoclasts were making a both/and into an either/or, requiring a choice between the Gospels [as written] and the icons. But if the Gospels and the cross were to be revered, the icons were also: "If the one is worthy of honor, the other is worthy of honor also." Since the content of Scripture and that of the icon were identical, "why do you worship the book and spit upon the picture?"[19]

The iconoclasts have clearly elevated the sense of hearing over the sense of sight; it is either/or. The iconophiles, however, insisted on both/and. God's salvation comes to us through ears and eyes. Here the iconophiles have a powerful argument, one that we can make in our own time. Preaching in our time, to be specific, may rightly appeal to ears and to eyes. We, too, must be cautioned about worshiping the book/word/ear and spitting on the picture! God created us with all of our senses, and God can use each and every one of our senses as a means to touch us with divinity. As John of

Damascus put it, the God who created matter has become matter for our salvation.

Theological Motifs

Besides using biblical passages to support their argument for the use of icons, the iconophiles developed certain theological motifs. The first of these themes, already touched on through the biblical texts, was the creation theme. Other prominent motifs were the incarnation of Jesus and the ability of finite matter to communicate the infinite.

God's Good Creation

John of Damascus could make a case for matter because he believed the Genesis story that God created matter and called it "good." This is a theological argument for the use of images and icons. Matter has been hallowed by its creation—and by its redemption: "For the creation waits with eager longing for the revealing of the children of God . . . [because] the creation itself will be set free from its bondage to decay" (Romans 8:19, 21). The creation will be redeemed!

In the context of philosophical dualism, it was maintained that humans sin because of the creation. Creation, or matter, ensnares us and locks us in a physical world far removed from spirit. That is our problem; escape from matter is our solution. The creation stories in Genesis, however, assert just the opposite. The creation is good, not evil, and it has fallen because of human sin. Salvation, therefore, is not escape from creation. Salvation comes to humans through the creation and frees us from our bondage to enable us to live lives of love and human fellowship on the good earth God created for us.

Neil Macgregor indicates that the view of creation as "good" stands as the primary argument against iconoclasms old and new: "Because God had chosen to make man 'in his image', it must be permissible for men in their turn to make images. Since Christ was incarnate as man, it was proper to show him as man."[20]

The case for the goodness of creation needs to be made very strongly. It is absolutely clear that a leading argument for the iconoclasts was the philosophical dualism that denigrated the creation. If the creation (matter) is evil, then there is no way to justify the artistic impulse of human creations. Icons and images are labeled as evil because they are matter. In direct contrast, the iconophiles refuse to believe that matter is evil. They criticize dualism for not being biblical teaching. The Bible teaches that the creation is good—indeed, very good! God's creative power has given us a good world that can bear God into our midst in Jesus Christ and that can be used artistically to enhance God's matter-full coming.

Incarnation

It is, of course, the very goodness of creation that makes incarnation possible. "And the Word became flesh and lived among us, and we have seen his glory, the glory as of a father's only son, full of grace and truth" (John 1:14). God can become human in the good stuff of creation! Neil Macgregor puts the case simply: "Unlike Muslims and Jews, Christians (or at least the early Christians) have *seen* their God; for Christianity is the religion of the Word made flesh, and, largely as a consequence, it is also a religion of the image."[21]

There is a formula here worth remembering. Protestantism has largely defined itself as a religion of the Word. This "Word" has come to mean primarily the Bible. But it is not the case that the Word of God became Bible. The Word of God became flesh. One could see this flesh with one's eyes. Christianity, as Macgregor puts it, is a religion of the image. *Seeing Salvation*, the title of Macgregor's book, was the order of the day for the first Christians. They saw him first with their eyes. Later on they heard him speak with their ears.

In his book *Imago Dei*, Jaroslav Pelikan devotes an entire chapter in his discussion of the iconoclastic controversy to the "Divine Made Human," that is, to the incarnation. More important, he argues that the conclusions reached through this debate were based primarily on theological reasoning. These theological reasons are as sound in the twenty-first century as they were in the eighth and ninth centuries. In the Eastern controversies, icons were derided as pagan idolatry. Visible gods were false gods. The Byzantine argument in reply was based on the doctrine of the incarnation, summarized here by Pelikan:

> The dogma of the person of Jesus Christ, as this had been codified by the ecumenical councils and the creeds, was to

supply the fundamental justification for the Christian icons in the church. . . . The Incarnation of Christ, as divinity made human, did make it possible for Byzantine theology to affirm the validity of aesthetics and of representational religious art, but in the process it also transformed both art and aesthetics into something they had never quite been before.[22]

Pelikan tracks two keys to the theological arguments of the iconophiles. These keys, he writes, are that Christ is "in two natures" and that Christ "has existence as a person." The two natures of the one Christ cannot be separated. The incarnation therefore gives us a reality that can be iconized. The incarnate God was a God who was *circumscribable*. The Eastern argument was that although you can't circumscribe an invisible God, the incarnation gives us a God who can be circumscribed. God had provided an icon of God. What is at stake here is the fullness of the two natures of Christ. If Christ is fully human, he can be iconized.[23]

The fullness of the humanity of Jesus is precisely the fullness that is unfathomable and unacceptable to those with a philosophical mind-set of dualism between God and human, divine and earthly, spirit and matter. John of Damascus understood the fullness of the humanity of Jesus versus the many christological heresies of his age. Since God is flesh in Jesus, John wrote, "Go ahead and image him in icons and present him for viewing, as one who wanted to be viewed. . . . [John lists the events in Jesus' life that can be iconized]—go ahead and describe all of these, both in words and in colors, both in books and in pictures!"[24]

Incarnation language can also take on the image of light: "The true light, which enlightens everyone, was coming into the world" (John 1:9). Light, of course, is another reference to the sense of sight:

> As Word, [Christ] was still there to be heard and obeyed; but as Light, he was now there to be seen as well—and therefore visualized, also in the form of an icon. Through the Incarnation, then, the visual had finally been rehabilitated, rescued from the service of idols, and restored to the worship as one who was . . . "Light of Light, true God from true God."[25]

The nimbus (halo of light) in many icons connects the image in the icon to Jesus, the Light of the world. When the light comes into the world, our sense of sight is redeemed. We can now see our Savior.

Our being is transformed by light. We see our salvation, and our beings are enlightened: "God is light and in him there is no darkness at all" (1 John 1:5).

Like Pelikan, Jeremy Begbie has observed that a full understanding of the incarnation is linked to justification of icons: "It is especially instructive to notice that those who were reluctant to accept that Christ was God incarnate were often also opponents of icons."[26] He adds that this denial of Christ's full humanity persisted for centuries.

Discussions of the incarnation have been tied to dialogue with christological questions. Pelikan notes that christological issues came noticeably to the fore in the ninth century in the Eastern church's debates over icons. He explains, "The central issue in the christological argument over the icons, therefore, was the question whether it was possible or permissible to 'circumscribe' . . . Jesus Christ."[27] The answer from the iconophiles was that *because of the incarnation,* it was possible to circumscribe Jesus. Humans had seen and touched this God-made-flesh. Icons and images were means of circumscribing God. You could paint a picture of this God. You could craft an icon of this God.

Communicating the Infinite

Another theological motif behind the arguments of the iconophiles was their belief that concrete matter could communicate to humans the presence of the infinite God. Such a theological statement was countercultural. In the world of the Eastern church, the philosophical context was dualism in its many forms. In contrast to the dualists' belief in an infinite, unbridgeable gap between the infinite and the finite, the iconophiles asserted that the infinite God had become finite in the incarnation of God in Jesus Christ. From that Christology, writes Pelikan, they "used the relation between the human and divine in Christ as an epitome of the dialectic between finite and infinite, as this dialectic manifested itself, for example, in the relation of the earthly and heavenly elements in the Eucharist."[28] In other words, the iconophiles' understanding of the two natures of Christ informed their understanding of the relationship between the infinite and the finite, including the way it is expressed in the Eucharist. The finite stuff of bread and wine is a means through which the infinite God can be present in our midst. The ability of the finite to communicate the infinite undergirded belief in the sacraments as a means ("means of grace") whereby God touches humans. Likewise, according to Begbie, Orthodox Christians and many others experienced icons not only as "witness to the process of transformation made possible by the incarnation," but also as "a means through which this process is effected in and experienced by the worshiper."[29]

Note the affinity between sacraments and icons. Sacraments and icons alike mediate the infinite God for the life of the finite believer. They mediate God's divinizing presence. To understand the mediating power of icons for the Eastern church, consider this ancient statement expressing the Orthodox understanding of salvation: "God became human so that humans might become divine." This formula also undergirds a *Christus Victor* model of the work of God for humans, in which Christ, infinite and finite, wins the victory over all the forces arrayed against life. Atonement is deification, the escape from corruption, as finite humans are divinized through the mediation of the infinite God present through finite means. This basic theology of the Eastern church is the heart of their understanding of salvation and icons' mediating power. In Orthodox churches, writes Dyrness, art "was meant to lift the soul toward the contemplation of God." A worshiper praying before an icon would be inspired "to love and imitate the one portrayed, that is to turn away from a worldly love toward a purer love of God. . . . [Images] became bearers of this reality."[30]

A common critique of the Eastern church's use of images is that such practice can easily cross over into superstition. As we will consider more fully in chapter 3, images most certainly can mean many different things to many different people. The Orthodox theologians were aware of such temptations and crafted careful understandings of images to avoid superstition and idolatry. They took care to distinguish between the image (the icon) and the person the icon depicts. "'For the honour rendered to the image goes to its prototype, and the person who venerates an icon venerates the person represented on it.'"[31]

Simply put, an image is a *means* of grace and not an *end* in itself. Through an icon, as through means, the infinite touches the finite.

In his wonderful and brief book titled *The Dwelling of the Light: Praying with Icons of Christ*, Rowan Williams touches on this subject. Williams speaks of the energy of God that is always radiating through the human nature of Jesus. An icon of Jesus, therefore, is to be understood as a center of radiating light and force moving out from Jesus toward the human subject. Williams explains that the defenders of icons always understood that icons worked in this way as a kind of gateway for God. The one who prays with or meditates upon an icon needs to allow the self to be worked upon by God. It is God who is looking at you through the icon. In, with, and under (to use words from Martin Luther) the icon, one becomes aware that one is present to God and that God is present and working God's grace. The icon is finite, but this finite icon is a means for the presence of the Infinite One.

In theological terms, the Eastern concept of divinization—God became human that humans might become divine—is called theosis. In recent years, a school of Finnish theologians have strive to demonstrate that Martin Luther, in particular, exhibited an understanding of theosis in his writings. In a recent book collecting their results, *Union with Christ: The New Finnish Interpretation of Luther*, one of the authors sets forth the basic premise: "Finnish Luther research has come to the conclusion that Luther's idea of the presence of Christ in faith can form a basis for treating the question of divinization. The Lutheran understanding of the indwelling of Christ implies a real participation in God and is analogous to the orthodox doctrine of participation in God, or *theosis*."[32]

Preaching That Participates in God

What implications does this iconic theology have for the *content* of preaching? Without entering into an extensive discussion of the Finnish research, I will make a few comments on what might be called "theotic preaching," hoping to provoke some new ways of thinking about preaching.

One of the Finnish theologians writing in *Union with Christ* says this of Luther's views:

> [Luther] claims that if the person of Christ and that of the believer are separated from each other in the *locus* of justifica-

tion, salvation is still within the framework of the order of the law.... [Quoting Luther:] *When it comes to justification, therefore, if you divide Christ's person from your own, you are in the Law; you remain in it and live in yourself, which means that you are dead in the sight of God and damned by the Law.*[33]

I am particularly struck by Luther's words "if you divide Christ's person from your own, you are in the Law." From this remark, it is clear that when preaching divides divine agency (God acting for us) from human agency (our response to God), we are preaching law but not gospel. Theologically, the Christ who is *for* us is separated from the Christ who is *in* us, so Christ remains outside of us. We are inside ourselves. We are the human agents. We are responsible for a response to divine action on our behalf. The problem for preaching arises when the focal aim of preaching is human agency. When we preachers seek to convince our listeners that they must act in response to divine agency, they are to follow and obey. They are to live up to the quality of mercy shown. They are to repent and put their lives right.

Our list could go on. The point is that when preaching divides divine agency from human agency, we find ourselves preaching primarily the "law" to the human agent. In my experience of listening to and reading sermons, I must say that most of these sermons are addressed to human agency. How very different preaching would sound if its reality were primarily an instrument of divine presence, in which we proclaim our finite words in such a way that the infinite Christ comes to the believer through our words. Preaching of this sort is sacramental in character—a means of grace. It is theosis in action. Dietrich Bonhoeffer understood preaching in just this way:

> The proclaimed word has its origin in the incarnation of Jesus Christ.... The proclaimed word is the incarnate Christ himself. As little as the incarnation is the outward shape of God, just so little does the proclaimed word present the outward form of a reality; rather it is the thing itself. The preached Christ is both the Historical One and the Present One.... The proclaimed word is not a medium of expression for something else ... but rather it is the Christ himself walking through his congregation as the Word.[34]

How might one describe this type of preaching? Let me list some ways of trying to imagine how theotic preaching might be expressed and experienced:

Theotic preaching . . .
• brings Christ as grace and gift into the human heart.
• mediates God's indwelling in the believer.
• is an instrument for the divinization of the believer.
• transforms human agency.
• gives birth to new hearts within us.
• mediates union with God in Christ.
• donates Christ to us.
• is the "real presence" of Christ "for us" and "in us."
• fills the hearer with God.
• creates our participation in God.

However we attempt to say it, the goal of theotic preaching would be as a servant to divine agency as that agency takes up residence in the human heart. Preaching would focus on mediating divine agency, rather than urging human agents to change their own lives.

Preaching by telling stories and making use of visual images can be theotic preaching. When preaching "thinks in stories," that is, by telling stories, it works toward the listener's participation in the story. This is true most particularly when we tell the biblical stories. The story of the prodigal son can serve as an example. When we tell that story, in contrast to explaining the story (for example, sorting it into parts 1, 2, and 3), we have a reasonable right to expect God to work through the hearing of the story. When we tell this story in such a way that listeners are engaged, we can hope that when the son experiences the good news from the father—"He was lost and is found; he was dead and is alive again"—we experience the good news as well. When the hearer participates in the life of God in the story, there is a real possibility that the work of God is *experienced* in the life of the hearer. Divine agency is at work through such a sermon. Theosis is a possibility. Hearers' lives are filled with God!

Thinking in picture has similar possibilities. When we use visual images in the course of our preaching, we are utilizing the finite image/icon/picture for infinite ends. Through seeing with our eyes, we can receive the coming of God into our lives. The finite does communicate the infinite. That is the Eastern conviction behind images. The infinite God can use the good sense of sight that God created as a means of God's presence within our very being. Eyes and ears are means of grace. Eyes and ears are means through which God can divinize the human. Divine agency takes place through that which we see. Theosis is a possibility!

In my previous works on preaching, I have urged preachers to use proclamatory language at the heart of the sermon. Think of proclamation as the heart of the sermon. This is what you walked into the pulpit to announce! Proclamation needs to facilitate God's speaking to the congregation through first- or second-person, present tense language. The message of the prodigal son's story, for example, is not a lesson about forgiveness. "Here is what we learn about in today's story." No! Let God speak. Create conditions for theosis. The proclamation should sound something like this: "What God is saying to you today through this story is, 'You were lost, and I found you. You were dead, and I have made you alive. Rise and live your lives as the person I created you to be, as the person I come to recreate you to be.'" Proclamation announces a promissory event of God. God's Word is a creative word. It creates what it announces (see Isaiah 55:10–11). It is a word that can make humans divine! Thus, the theotic sermon focuses on divine agency, not human responsive agency.

Eyes and Ears

In defending the use of icons, the Eastern church sought a complementary understanding of eyes and ears. We normally think of preaching as having to do exclusively with ears. Icons and images, however, introduce eyes into our way of thinking about preaching. In Pelikan's analysis, seeing has temporal priority over hearing. In Jesus' ministry, for example, people often first saw Jesus with their eyes. What they later heard through their ears from Jesus or from his followers helped to give meaning to what their eyes had seen. The visual sense has also been rehabilitated through the incarnation of God's Son. We see with new eyes. We are enlightened.

The Eastern church had what Pelikan might call an evangelism ap-proach that worked through the sense of sight. As the disciples first saw Christ and then heard the preaching of the gospel, "now it was the icons that . . . served as the visible basis for the oral-aural message."[35] The way this worked when a Christian wanted to present the gospel to a pagan was that the Christian "would take his friend to church and show him the icons there, so that the pagan would ask about these figures and in this way open himself to the Christian message."[36]

In its liturgical rites, too, the Eastern church moves from eye to ear. When worshipers enter the church building and the liturgical service, there is much for the eye to see. Icons are powerfully present along with other artistic forms. After the worshipers have seen, then comes the time for the ear. The scripture is read and heard. Preaching is spoken and heard. In this process, the worship involves more than one human sense in a holistic experience. We can regain some of this majesty of worship in our time through liturgy and preaching that appeal to both eye and ear. Indeed, the complementary nature of eye and ear lies at the center of my argument. It is vital in our time to recapture the holism of human senses in order to proclaim the good news of the divine agent who intends to turn human agency, with its proclivity to sin, inside out!

According to Pelikan, liturgical practice and doctrine are what triumphed over the iconoclasts. He refers to this as the *melody of theology.* "Speaking of the role of the icons in worship, Nicephorus asserted that they conveyed 'theological knowledge' about a divine reality that transcended all being. 'They are . . . expressive of the silence of God, exhibiting in themselves the ineffability of a mystery that transcends being.'"[37] Therein lies the melody of theology!

Reformed Iconoclasm

As I noted at the close of chapter 1, on the eve of the Reformation, there was a perceived imbalance between the visual and the auditory. The visual (the use of images, icons, works of art, statues, etc.) was everywhere. There are few boundaries for the superstitions that can arise from that which the eye beholds. Thus, the ecclesiastical world was filled with pious frauds, myriads of "true crosses" and the like. Something had to change.

The need for change was demonstrated in both the Roman Catholic and Protestant worlds. In the response to the Reformation made by Roman Catholicism at the Council of Trent, Margaret Miles notes the council members took up the question of images by defining proper uses for images and prohibiting subject matter that tended to "cause or reinforce dangerous dogmatic errors."[38] This Catholic reform intended to restore balance to visual and auditory modes of perceiving, rather than emphasizing one mode so much that the other would be excluded.[39] The Catholic reform was not nearly as radical as the reform movements set loose in some Protestant contexts. The Protestant reform, as we shall see, sought to eliminate images from the lives of Christians. The Protestant Reformers made their appeal exclusively to the auditory sense, to the word alone. As I have already indicated, balance is my own way of participating in this debate. Throughout this book, I plead for a well-balanced presentation of the Christian faith, using word and image, appealing to ear and eye. However, Protestant iconoclasm upsets this equilibrium in its spiritual appeal to the word alone.

In *War against Idols*, Carlos M. N. Eire describes the difference between the visual world of the medieval period and the new thrust of the "Reformed" Reformation as a difference in emphasis. In Eire's interpretation, the visual medieval world emphasized a religion of immanence: God was present for humans in this world through the mediation of what the eyes could see in an icon or an image. With the Reformed movement, writes Eire, "The religion of immanence was replaced by the religion of transcendence."[40] He cites as a central Reformed principle that the finite is incapable of communicating the infinite (*finitum non est capax infiniti*). A religion of immanence, therefore, is an impossibility. The infinite God cannot be immanent to humans through finite means. Therefore, the Reformed movement made radical changes: "Aiming to do away with any practice that compromised the 'spiritual' worship commanded by God, the Reformed launched a vigorous attack on all external objects of devotion that had previously been charged with religious value."[41] Theology, in this case, led to concrete results on the streets and in the churches of parts of Europe. Wandel provides a vivid description:

In the sixteenth century, in dozens of towns and villages, otherwise ordinary people—parish clergy, bakers, carpenters, gardeners, most employed and most of them citizens—broke into local churches and smashed up or burned thousands of long-beloved, familiar, treasured objects: altars, altar retables, crucifixes, carved and painted triptychs and diptychs, panel painting, architectural and free-standing sculptures, chalices, patens, candlesticks, and oil lamps.[42]

Eire calls this "redefinition of the sacred" the watershed that separated the Reformed Reformation from both the Lutheran Reformation and the Catholic attempts at reform.

What was quite different about this iconoclastic revolt was the broad range of people involved. The debates of the eighth- and ninth-century Eastern church were largely confined to edicts from emperors and debates among theologians. The Reformed revolt was different. Everyday people committed everyday havoc in the churches. This iconoclastic rebellion began in Wittenberg, Germany, and then moved to Switzerland, France, and the Low Countries and Scotland. Almost all the actors in this movement were men. Their intellectual leaders included Erasmus, Andreas Bodenstein von Karlstadt, Ulrich Zwingli, and John Calvin.

Erasmus: Dualistic Thinker

The Dutch scholar Erasmus, writes Carlos Eire, should get the credit for "the Reformed Protestant attitude toward worship." The reason is that Erasmus originated what became a new way in which Christians interpreted the relationship between spiritual and material. Eire explains:

> Erasmus insisted that the inner life of the spirit was superior to any material or formal considerations; and this principle formed the basis for his interpretation of the nature of worship. . . . From the very start Erasmus proposes a piety that has little need for material objects of worship. . . . [Eire quotes Erasmus] "You can only establish perfect piety when you turn away from visible things, which are for the most part either imperfect or of themselves indifferent, and you seek instead the invisible, which corresponds to the highest part of human nature."[43]

In this quotation, Erasmus marks a very clear distinction between the spiritual world and the material world, the invisible world and the visible world. As this type of dualism is grounded in the assumptions of Hellenistic philosophy, Erasmus appears to share that philosophical heritage.

According to Eire, dualism informed Reformed thinking as well, but Erasmus did not go far enough. Erasmus apparently was indifferent to the "material piety" of the medieval church. He could even talk of pictures as a kind of silent poetry that often captured his emotional state better than words. The weak in faith, therefore, might need pictures. If pictures and icons were to be done away with, said Erasmus, then something better would need to be put in their place. Eire concludes, therefore, that though Erasmus laid the groundwork for Reformed thinking on the nature of the relationship between the spiritual and the material worlds, he is certainly not the source of the attack on icons for the Reformed: "When the images and the Mass were abolished in Basel, Erasmus fled, unable to accept the intolerance he had engendered in spite of himself."[44]

Karlstadt: Leader of the Attack

Erasmus's ideas about the dualism between spirit and matter were an important influence on the German theologian, Andreas Bodenstein von Karlstadt of Wittenberg. According to Carlos Eire, Karlstadt initiated the main Protestant attack on Roman Catholic idolatry. Eire writes that Karlstadt cited Jesus' statement that God is a spirit (see John 6:63) to argue against the value of physical elements of worship: "Material elements are unable to convey spiritual benefits. . . . Images serve no good religious purpose. The reason for this, he says, is that images are bound to the flesh and cannot transcend it."[45]

Karlstadt justified his iconoclasm by writing a treatise titled *On the Abolition of Images,* the first major Protestant pamphlet on this topic. In his pamphlet, he enunciates three basic theses:

1. The presence of images in churches and houses of God is wrong and contrary to the second commandment.
2. Carved and painted idols on the altars are even more devilish and dangerous.

3. It is good, necessary and praiseworthy to abolish images and to give to scripture its right and judgment.[46]

On the basis of his theories, Karlstadt led his followers in Wittenberg to attack the churches and cleanse them of idols and images. He saw it as the duty of the laity to remove idols in this way. This duty flowed from the divine command against images as stipulated by the second commandment. Karlstadt's motivations resemble those of the iconoclasts of the Eastern church, who also quoted the second commandment condemning idolatry. They also share a dualism in their understanding of spiritual and material matters. They insist the finite is incapable of bearing the infinite.

At the time Karlstadt asserted his leadership in Wittenberg, Martin Luther had appeared before the Diet of Worms and been whisked off to the Wartburg Castle by his secular prince for protection from the Roman authorities. Luther heard of Karlstadt's work and left theWartburg to examine the ministry in Wittenberg, the town in which he lived and taught. Upon his return to Wittenberg, Luther preached a series of sermons, known as the *Invocavit* Sermons or Luther's Eight Wittenberg Sermons, indicting Karlstadt for his liturgical and iconoclastic practices. In confronting Karlstadt's revolution this way, Luther showed a lack of concern for reformation that focused on distinguishing the spiritual and the material.[47] We will look at Luther's response to Karlstadt later in this chapter, but for now we simply note differences in the Reformation era between iconoclastic theology and Luther's theology. These viewpoints lead to very different conclusions regarding the use of visuals in preaching for our time.

Zwingli: Toward True Worship

Ulrich Zwingli was a Reformation leader who lived and worked in Zurich, Switzerland. Like Karlstadt, he was influenced by the work of Erasmus, and like Erasmus, he can be considered a humanist. Zwingli abhorred the religious practices he encountered in Zurich:

> Men kneel, bow, and remove their hats before them [idols and images]; candles and incense are burned before them; men name them after the saints whom they represent; men kiss them; men adorn them with gold and jewels; men designate them with the appellation merciful or gracious; men seek con-

solation merely from touching them, or even hope to acquire remission of sins thereby.[48]

Zwingli's protest refers to the dominance of the visual, which was a characteristic of medieval Christianity.

Zwingli attacked this visual sense with the use of scripture, with God's Word, and with the dominance of the auditory sense. Scripture was the major influence upon Zwingli. The commands of scripture were for him the blueprint for how worship in the churches should be practiced. He argued that only scripture could determine the substance and practice of Christianity. The good people of Zurich accepted the authority of scripture as Zwingli set it forth. They, in turn, legislated the Reformation in Zurich and led the revolution against idols during the years 1522 to 1526.

Zwingli's views on idols tapped into the already deep feelings of the people in Zurich. They had their own reasons for objecting to idolatry. According to Lee Palmer Wandel, people believed it was better to give money to the poor than to pay artists and craftspeople to make images. In addition, they objected to the rents and tithes the church imposed on them for purchasing the images. Furthermore, after hearing the teaching of iconoclasts, some concluded that the smashing of images would be credited to them by God as a good work. Responding to the complaints of clergy and laity on the matter of images, the town council of Zurich issued the following resolution:

> Since, our gracious Lord Burgermeister, council, and Great council, were informed through the Holy Word and in the past discussions among their own and other learned men, and since nothing else has been discovered, than that the Almighty God has forbidden the images or idols to be made, and recognizes no worship to be done them. . . . [therefore our conclusion is] to do away with the images or idols in all places where they are worshiped, so that many turn themselves from the idols to the living true God through our Lord Jesus Christ. . . . And the goods and expenses that have been laid upon these images should be turned to the poor needy human beings, who are a true image of God.[49]

Responding to this official legislation, the people of Zurich proceeded to cleanse the city of artwork devoted to God. They painted the walls of the churches white so that none of the paintings of the medieval church were visible any longer. All the altars, paintings, and crucifixes were removed and destroyed. Miles writes, "By Sunday, July 3, 1524, scarcely a statue, a painting, a crucifix, a votive lamp, a reliquary, a shrine, or image or decoration of any sort was to be seen anywhere in the Zurich churches."[50] The Reformed Church had become a reality in Zurich.

Zwingli led not so much through his direct actions, but through his teachings. His core convictions included the dangers of material things to the life of the spirit, the second commandment's prohibition of images, and a determination to reform worship so that it would be worship as commanded by God. For Zwingli, as for John Calvin (discussed next), true worship was at the heart and center of the Reformation, in contrast to Luther's central concern: finding a gracious God. According to Eire, "Zwingli asserts that the cause of error in religion is man's dependence on created things, and his penchant for placing trust in them," so his objection to images in churches arises from "his opposition to any objects of faith (inner or outer) that usurp God in worship."[51]

However, in this zeal to reform worship, an elitism of the word developed. Margaret Miles accords this elitism of the word to both Lutherans and Reformed: "Auditory participation in worship represented simultaneously a new relation to the language of liturgy. . . . The focal point of services in Lutheran and Reformed churches was the preaching of the word."[52] William Dyrness puts the matter this way: "The prime symbol of true belief [for Zwingli] is the word, invisible and heard; the prime symbol of false belief is the image, visible and seen."[53]

The changes of the Reformation therefore moved the church from one imbalance to another. The emphasis on the visual before the Reformation was pushed into the opposite imbalance: domination by the auditory sense. That change was a signal of the end of the medieval world. It marked the beginning of a modern era in which "people come to privilege 'subjective consciousness' as the normal human activity."[54] This privileging of subjective consciousness is part of the reason that many Protestant voices today reject out of hand the use of visuals in preaching, the recovery of the visible and the "seen" in the homiletical task. The power of the concept of "Word alone" has more or less permeated Protestant theology into our present age. Such voices are true to a part of the Reformation heritage.

Calvin: Purifier of Worship

John Calvin shared and shaped the Protestant protests against images, idols, and the predominance of the visual sense. Where Pope Gregory the Great called images "the books of the uneducated," Calvin retorts, "'Whatever men learn of God in images is futile, indeed false; the prophets totally condemn the notion that images stand in the place of books.' By contrast, it is through the pure preaching of the Word that one comes to proper faith."[55] For Calvin, belief in the Word, purely preached, was not only a higher way but also a more direct path to the truth. This argument expresses a very strong sense of the total effectiveness of the pure and bare preaching of the Word. This totally inner way provides a spiritual connection directly, not through visible means, between God and human.

The issue of idolatry was central to Calvin's conversion and transformation. He stood firmly against all the "superstitions of popery." For Calvin, everything was at stake in the reformation of worship life. He was, therefore, an ardent opponent of Roman Catholic worship, which was so corrupted, as he saw it, by idolatry. Calvin viewed idolatry as the antithesis of religion, which must provide "spiritual worship," that is, "worship devoid of trust in material props or humanly devised ceremonies; and worship that has been commanded by God."[56]

Carlos Eire sets forth the fundamentals of Calvin's theology, built upon Calvin's definition of creation's purpose: "for man to know God and to glorify him by worship and obedience." Eire explains, "Knowledge of God and worship of God are inseparable: One cannot come to know God without yielding some worship to Him. . . . Calvin's primary concern in his struggle against Catholic piety was to defend the glory of the God who is 'entirely other,' who transcends all materiality. . . . whose reality is inaccessible."[57] Glorifying God is Calvin's reason for attacking the images he views as idolatrous:

> Calvin's attack on idolatry was an effort to restore God's primary dignity among human beings. . . . Calvin's attack on Roman Catholic "idolatry" is a condemnation of the improper mixing of spiritual and material in worship—an affirmation

of the principle [that the finite cannot convey the infinite]. It is also an indictment of man's attempt to domesticate God and to rob him of his glory—and affirmation of the principle *soli Deo gloria*.[58]

Commentators on Calvin's theology are quick to point out that Calvin was not operating out of a dualistic system that condemns the materiality of the creation. Calvin is not a Gnostic! What makes images idolatrous is not their materiality, but rather "man himself, who is impudent enough to seek divinity on his own terms instead of the Creator's. Man reverses the order of divine reality, expecting to find the Creator in the created. As long as man remains embroiled in the material level of his own existence, and is satisfied with his own corrupt being, he is immersed in the darkest error."[59] Thus, compared with God, humans are worthless, and their goal is to transcend the created world. The way for a person to receive truth and eternal life, according to Calvin, is to "regard the world as worthless."[60] Relying on Carlos Eire's discussion of Calvin, we can summarize Calvin's major contributions to the Reformed theology of transcendence in terms of three points:

1. The blame for idolatry is not to be placed on God and the material world but upon the sinful human person. Not the material world in general, but rather humans and human nature are corrupt and evil.[61]

2. More than his Reformed colleagues, Calvin focused centrally on worship: "'True piety begets true confession.' This is enormously significant. One may even argue that it becomes the fundamental defining characteristic of Calvinism."[62]

3. Calvin offered an analysis of reverential acts that effectively removed all material religious objects from the worship experience.

Martin Luther's Response

Responding directly to the radical reforming work Karlstadt was carrying out in Luther's hometown of Wittenberg, Martin Luther in 1525 wrote a pamphlet titled *Against the Heavenly Prophets in the Matter of Images and Sacraments.* One of Luther's first arguments in the pamphlet centers on "good works." Luther saw Karlstadt commanding people by scripture to the task of smashing idols, and Luther interpreted this as the commanding of a "good work." For Luther, this emphasis on works could lead to no good:

> Fame, vain glory and a new monkery would thereby be achieved, as happens in all works, but the conscience would in no way be helped. . . . [Karlstadt] stresses and emphasizes external works, let everyone be warned of him. Everyone should know that he has a perverted spirit that thinks only of murdering the conscience with laws, sin and works. . . . Something higher must be there to be absolved and comfort the conscience. This is the Holy Spirit, who is not acquired through breaking images or any other works, but only through the gospel and faith.[63]

Luther later goes on to call the breaking of images "a work of the law which has taken place without the Spirit and faith." For people who engage in such behavior, "it makes for pride of heart, as though they by such works had gained a special status before God."[64] When Karlstadt teaches the sinfulness of idols, writes Luther, he is making a "minor, external" issue into one that "burdens the conscience." He adds, "I would release and free consciences and the souls from sin, which is a truly spiritual and evangelical pastoral function while Karlstadt seeks to capture them with law and burden them with sin without cause."[65]

Luther then discusses images according to the law of Moses and according to the gospel. Luther's interpretation of Moses is a strict interpretation.

According to Moses, he asserts, the only images that are forbidden are images that are worshiped. Luther is one with Calvin in seeing idolatry as the key issue. Luther pushes hard on this point: "If one then can make and set up altars and special stones, so that God's commandment is not trespassed because worship is absent, then my image breakers must also let me keep, wear, and look at a crucifix or a Madonna, yes, even an idol's image, in full accord with the strictest Mosaic law, as long as I do not worship them."[66]

Another argument that Luther puts forward to dispute Karlstadt's tactics is his claim that Karlstadt's followers are smashing idols in a disorderly manner and without proper civil authority. This idea is paired with Luther's desire to speak evangelically of images. Although no one should be obligated to break images, nor should violence be used, "One is obligated, however, to destroy them with the Word of God, that is not with the law in a Karlstadtian manner, but with the gospel. This means to instruct and enlighten the conscience that it is idolatry to worship them, or to trust in them, since one is to trust alone in Christ."[67]

Luther is always distrustful of using the arguments of the law, even the law of Moses, against images. According to Luther, Moses is only for the Jews: "We say further, that all such Mosaic teachers deny the gospel, banish Christ, and annul the whole New Testament. I now speak as a Christian for Christians. For Moses is given to the Jewish people alone, and does not concern us Gentiles and Christians. We have our gospel and New Testament."[68] On this matter Calvin and Luther stand far apart. According to Carlos Eire, Calvin understood that the Old Testament's commands against idolatry were not just for the ancient Jews. Human nature, after all, is still the same, and Gentiles can easily fall into idolatry as the Israelites did.[69]

Although Luther has problems with the dominantly visual world of the church he was born into, he will not use the law as his basis of argument. He cites Paul in Galatians 5:3 for evidence that once you determine you must accept one item of the Mosaic law (circumcision in this case), you are bound to keep the whole law of Moses. Luther argues on the basis of the gospel. Idolatry is a matter of the human heart, and the gospel is preached to transform human hearts. According to Luther, that's how to get rid of idols. Hearts transformed by the work of the Holy Spirit through the gospel leave no haven for idols: "I approached the task of destroying images by first tearing them out of the heart through God's Word and making them worthless and despised. . . . For when they are no longer in the heart, they can do no harm when seen with the eyes."[70]

This pamphlet is Luther's attempt to create an evangelical approach to the matter of idols and images. It is clear from his arguments that Luther was not opposed to the use of images in principle. He was opposed to images that become idols and called for a transformation of the human heart through the preaching of the gospel. Toward the end of his pamphlet, Luther defends the use of pictures in the life of the church by noting that the Bible used in Germany by all parties contained a great many pictures:

> So now we would kindly beg them to permit us to do what they themselves do. . . . Pictures contained in these books we would paint on walls for the sake of remembrance and better understanding, since they do no more harm on walls than in books. . . . Yes, would to God that I could persuade the rich and the mighty that they would permit the whole Bible to be painted on houses, on the inside and outside, so that all can *see* it. That would be a Christian work.[71]

And confessing his own need for images, Luther makes the case that word and images play a complementary role in the inner workings of the Christian:

> God desires to have his works heard and read, especially the passion of our Lord. But it is impossible for me to hear and bear it in mind without forming mental images of it in my heart. For whether I will or not, when I hear of Christ, an image of a man hanging on a cross takes form in my heart, just as the reflection of my face naturally appears in the water when I look into it. If it is not a sin but good to have the image of Christ in my heart, why should it be a sin to have it in my *eyes?*[72]

Neil Macgregor reminds us that Luther made use of his artist friend, Lucas Cranach, as Lutheranism's quasi-official artist. Cranach's son, Lucas the Younger, created an altarpiece for the church in Wittenberg (see page 16 above) that expressed, even preached, Luther's theology. Macgregor writes, "The altarpiece is, as Luther would have wished, *the word made paint:* and while every picture may tell a story, only a particular kind of picture can preach a sermon. The sermon here is on the Lutheran doctrine of salvation."[73]

Another concrete use of visual images by Luther was the Bible he published in 1522. This Bible included twenty-two woodcuts illustrating biblical events. Here, too, Luther juxtaposed the written word with the word made paint (perhaps we should say "woodcut") in order to appeal to multiple senses. It is clear that Luther's opposition to the use of images of various types was a concern for the idolatry such images could occasion in the human heart, certainly not the use of "painted words" in the lives of the people and in the ministry of the church.

Therefore, Martin Luther was not an iconoclast in the sense I have been using that word. The Protestant Reformers of the sixteenth century were divided over the way in which the Reformation should respond to the visually dominated ecclesial world into which they were born. Theological differences led Calvin and Luther down different paths. Calvin was focused on true worship that is "spiritual" and commanded by scripture. His understanding of spirit and scripture led him, along with the other Reformed leaders, to take a strong iconoclastic stand.

New Life for an Old Debate

In some ways, the Reformation-era views about images have continued an earlier debate, and opinions remain divided to this day. In the earlier discussion of the Eastern theologians who opposed iconoclasm, we identified three important theological motifs. Let us return to them in light of the Reformed and Lutheran thinking and then consider how these views persist in the church today.

Theological Motifs from the Reformers' Viewpoint

In contrast to the earlier dualistic arguments, Eire notes that the Reformed theologians had a positive view of the creation in general and matter in particular. Calvin is the most careful of the Reformed theologians in agreeing that creation is good and the problem with the material world is a human problem: "God's exalted position in relation to creation is disregarded by the idolater. Those who worship falsely, reverse the proper order of the universe, placing the material over the spiritual."[74] Humans must refrain from making icons, not because all matter is evil, but because humans are evil and their icons are idols. This theology essentially forbids material artistic creations in the church's life.

The second theological motif we noted earlier had to do with incarnation of God in the flesh of Jesus Christ. Because Jesus was wholly God and wholly human, God is circumscribable. Elements of Reformed theology reject this conclusion, saying instead that

God is spirit and cannot be circumscribed. This view may be most clearly articulated in the christological formula of Ulrich Zwingli. This view, called *alloeosis,* asserts that there is no intermingling of the two natures of Christ. The divine and human natures remain complete and separate from each other. Luther's very different view, called *communicatio idiomatum,* was that the two natures of Christ totally interpenetrated each other. This christological difference is what led to the disagreement between Zwingli and Luther over the presence of Christ in the Lord's Supper, debated at the Colloquy of Marburg in 1529. Zwingli argued for the "spiritual" presence of Christ in the Supper. The spiritual and the act of eating and drinking were not to be commingled. Luther argued for a "real presence" of Jesus Christ in, with, and under the very elements of bread and wine. Christ was present for humans in the actual chewing of the bread and swallowing of wine. This christological debate about the Supper is a clue that Luther and Zwingli also have different perspectives on the physical elements used in icons.

The third theological motif—that the finite is capable of communicating the infinite—means simply that the finite, material stuff of the earth is able to mediate the infinite God to finite humans. Calvin came to the opposite conclusion: the finite cannot communicate the infinite. Icons can only be idols, due to the evil of humans. In contrast, Martin Luther concurred with the Eastern theologians that the finite can communicate the infinite.

According to the Finnish school of Luther research that has rediscovered many affinities between the theology of Martin Luther and Eastern theology, Luther is in agreement with the East on each of the theological motifs that led the East to reject iconoclasm. In particular, Luther and John of Damascus have very similar theological positions. Each believes in the goodness of the created world. Each believes that God was incarnate deep in the flesh of humanity. This understanding is apparent in Luther's explanation of the first article of the Apostles' Creed in his *Small Catechism*:

> I believe that God has created me together with all creatures. God has given me and still preserves my body and soul: eyes, ears, and all limbs and senses; reason and all mental faculties. In addition God daily and abundantly provides shoes and clothing, food and drink, house and home, spouse and

children, fields, livestock, and all property—along with all the necessities and nourishment for this body and life.

With this explanation, Luther affirms God's intimate earthly involvement in the daily life of the many creatures in God's good creation.

In his explanation to the second article of the Apostles' Creed, Luther affirms, with John of Damascus, the down-to-earth nature of the incarnation. Luther writes that the meaning of this article of the creed affirms the full humanity of Jesus: "I believe that Jesus Christ, true God, begotten of the Father in eternity, and also true human being, born of a Virgin Mary, is my Lord." The incarnation means that God in Jesus Christ is fully human. Luther emphasized the full participation of the divinity in the humanity of Jesus more strongly than many of the theologians of his age. Paul Althaus quotes Luther: "God has suffered; a man created heaven and earth; a man died; God who is from all eternity died; the boy who nurses at the breast of the Virgin Mary is the creator of all things. . . . Whoever wishes to think about or to meditate on God in a way that will lead him to salvation must subordinate everything else to the humanity of Christ."[75] Such a God is, indeed, circumscribable.

Finally, John of Damascus and Martin Luther each believe that the finite is capable of communicating the infinite. We see this dimension of Luther's theology also in his *Small Catechism*. Luther holds to a very *real presence* of God in the physical elements of the sacraments of Baptism and the Lord's Supper. In his explanations in the catechism, he asks how water and bread and wine can do such great things. Responding to his own question, he acknowledges that water alone or bread and wine alone cannot do such great things, but when these physical elements are used together with the words of God's promises, then they do great things. Faith trusts the word with the water. Faith trusts the word with bread and wine. Therefore, through these earthly elements, the holy God is physically present to persons of faith. Luther here anticipates the dualists of every age who want to separate the physical and the spiritual elements in the sacraments. There will be no merely "spiritual presence" of God in the sacramental life of the church, as far as Luther is concerned. God can use the stuff of God's creation as an instrument of God's presence for us. It is no stretch at all to believe that Luther would take a very similar approach to the whole matter of icons. Icons may also have a sacramental character when they are connected with God's word of promise. Both John and Luther believed that icons and images could play a vital role in the life of the church while warning against idolatrous usage of such works of art.

Protestants Today

Extending Calvin and Luther's sixteenth-century positions into a postmodern context would most probably lead us to very different conclusions about the use of visualization in preaching today. Even so, many Reformed theologians today support the use of visualization in worship and preaching. The recent books by William Dyrness and Jeremy Begbie are examples of Protestant writers who are seeking to recover the visual sense. Centuries-old theological claims concerning the infinite and the finite clearly do not dictate contemporary thinking on this matter for some. Conversely, many of my fellow Lutherans are not very supportive of using visualization in the preaching context. A formal agreement between some Lutheran and Reformed churches in America acknowledges differences of emphasis in our respective reformers and traditions and calls upon our churches to discuss theological differences, which are not church-dividing, in a spirit of mutual admonition and affirmation. Our churches have found a very healthy way for us to approach some of our differing theological emphases. I am hopeful that a constructive dialogue on the theological motifs we have noted here will help us all walk into a newly visual world.

In my research on this matter, I was often confronted with statements that the Protestant churches have a very skeptical view of the use of art and of the visual sense. Authors claim that Protestants value the word alone and elevate the sense of hearing over "words made paint" created for seeing. Robert Johnson's book on theology and film in the life of the church refers to "the Protestant suspicion of the image, its reverence for the rational word, and its concentration on redemption theology to the sometimes exclusion of creation theology," and the author calls for "a more adequate theology of image"[76] so the church can be more fully engaged in conversation with filmmakers and Hollywood. Similarly Margaret Miles writes of the Reformation's success in terms of "a language-oriented religion and culture." She says, "As people were gradually educated to attend more to the word than to visual images . . . the success of the Protestant reform in the creation of a new linguistic culture was assured. . . . Vision lost its centrality to religion as it became only incidentally engaged in worship and devotion."[77]

Having grown up in the Lutheran tradition, I had difficulty relating to statements such as these, though I knew in my bones there must be something to these claims because I have heard them time and again in Protestant circles. I had forgotten the iconoclastic nature of the Reformed branch of the sixteenth-century Reformation. As my research indicates, these claims for the dominance of the auditory sense to the near exclusion of the visual sense in understanding the means of salvation have very strong grounds in one part of the Reformation heritage. We have also seen, however, that Martin Luther was more iconophile than iconoclast. His thinking on this subject is remarkably parallel with that of John of Damascus. There are, therefore, Protestant voices strongly supportive of the sense of the visual.

Because the visual sense was dominant in a sometimes idolatrous manner on the eve of the Reformation, both Roman Catholic and Protestant reformers sought to address this imbalance. Roman Catholicism sought to reestablish an equilibrium between the ear and the eye in the church's life. Reformed Protestantism, on the other hand, sought to remove the sense of the eye and the use of earthly, material icons and images. On this matter, Martin Luther is closer to the reformers of Trent than to those in Geneva. Luther, too, sought an equilibrium of the auditory and visual senses in the worship life of the church. This is my position as well. I firmly believe that John of Damascus and Martin Luther provide us with all the theological arguments we need to justify the attempt to appeal to the visual dimension of humans, even in our preaching. The sons and daughters of the Reformation, Lutheran and Reformed, need each other today for mutual affirmation and admonition of views as we move forward in this endeavor. The Lutheran position clearly opens the way for appeals to our visual sense. The Reformed position reminds us of some very important theological dangers that can overtake us in such an enterprise. We must avoid idolatry and superstition at all costs.

In the next chapter, we will turn to a discussion of almost this exact topic as carried out in the history of Western philosophical thinking. There has been a centuries-long debate in these circles over the relative merit of poetry versus painting, to borrow a phrase from W. J. T. Mitchell's important book, *Iconology: Image, Text, Ideology.* Mitchell and others who join this debate declare that poetry has won this debate in intellectual circles. Words have consistently been declared more valuable than images.

Mitchell's correct assessment that poetry/words/ear are valued much more than painting/images/eye in philosophical circles creates a powerful word of caution to the use of painting/images/eye in the life of the church. As I think about debates on this subject in which I have been involved, it seems that this conclusion in the world of philosophical thinking has had a powerful and negating effect on the church's right and need to appeal to the sense of visualization, for example, in preaching. Along with Reformed Protestantism's iconoclasm, the philosophical dualism that values poetry over painting adds a twin stream of thought against the church's use of painting/images/eye. They argue that the church ought to value poetry/words/ear above all else. To explore that idea further, the next chapter turns to the philosophical world's discussion of poetry versus painting.

3

Poetry and Painting

ACCORDING TO THE preceding chapter's historical overview, church leaders until the Protestant Reformation struggled to find the proper balance between the visual and auditory senses in the presentation of the gospel message. When the visual sense dominated the auditory sense in the sixteenth century, both the Roman Catholic Church and the Reformed branch of the Protestant Reformation sought to redress this dominance. Also, the Reformation era included major iconoclastic controversies, during which certain church leaders severely restrained the sense of the visual.

The relation of the visual and auditory senses is not, however, a subject restricted to the church. A debate about the relative merits of visual and auditory, eye and ear, image and word, painting and poetry has long been taking place in the world of philosophy. That philosophical debate parallels the church's discussion. W. J. T. Mitchell, in *Iconology: Image, Text, Ideology,* has summarized the philosophers' discussion, and this chapter is based in part on his most helpful insights. This discussion is important for us because the results of this philosophical debate permeate our cultural presuppositions about the relative merits of poetry and painting.

Iconology:
Thinking about Images

Mitchell's book addresses the most basic questions about images: "What is an image?" and "What is the difference between images and words?"[1] In answering those questions, Mitchell presents two broad arguments:

(1) there is no *essential* difference between poetry and painting, no difference, that is, that is given for all time by the inherent nature of the media, the objects they represent, or the laws of the human mind; (2) there are always a number of differences in effect in a culture which allow it to sort out the distinctive qualities of its ensemble of signs and symbols.[2]

These arguments, writes Mitchell, simply continue an ages-old debate in intellectual circles. The relative merit of pictorial and linguistic signs has been the subject of many discussions in the history of human cultures, what Mitchell calls "a constant." He describes this as a kind of power struggle over how we will express meaning:

The history of culture is in part the story of a protracted struggle for dominance between pictorial and linguistic signs, each claiming for itself certain proprietary rights of a "nature" to which only it has access. . . . Why do we have this compulsion to conceive of the relations between words and images in political terms, as a struggle for territory, a context of rival ideologies? . . . [A short answer is] the relationship between word and images reflects, within the realm of representation, signification, and communication, the relations we posit between symbols and the world, signs and their meanings.[3]

Word and image have constantly been pitted against each other in human "culture wars." The issue is nothing less than how we interpret our world, how we assign meaning.

The most formidable defense of the distinct boundaries between poetry and painting is *Laocoon*, written by Gotthold Lessing. Lessing is cited with "ritual regularity" by those who take part in this particular aspect of the "culture war." Using the following chart by Lessing, Mitchell explicates the relative merits of painting and poetry. Lessing's chart is extremely important for grasping the nuances of perceived differences between the visual and the auditory worlds.[4]

Painting	Poetry
space	time
natural signs	arbitrary (man-made) signs
narrow space	infinite range
imitation	expression

Painting *(continued)*	Poetry
body	mind
external	internal
silent	eloquent
beauty	sublimity
eye	ear
feminine	masculine

It doesn't take long to see the many ways that poetry is favored over painting in this list. Note the value system at work. Mind is superior to body. The internal is superior to the external. The ear is superior to the eye. Masculine is superior to the feminine. And why be surprised? This is a list created by masculine thinkers. It reflects exactly the dualism we have asserted for the intellectual world of Greece and of all iconoclasts.

But does this chart really matter? According to Mitchell, Lessing's case is significant because it defines such a dominant way of thinking in the West: "Lessing rationalizes a fear of imagery that can be found in every major philosopher from Bacon to Kant to Wittgenstein, a fear not just of the 'idols' of pagan primitives, or of the vulgar marketplace, but of the idols which insinuate themselves into language and thought, the false models which mystify both perception and representation."[5] In addition, Mitchell explains, this Western iconoclasm reflects a kind of prejudice and exclusiveness:

> The idol then, tends to be simply an image overvalued by an *other*; by pagans and primitives; by children or foolish women; by Papists and ideologues. . . . The rhetoric of iconoclasm is thus a rhetoric of exclusion and domination, a caricature of the other as one who is involved in irrational, obscene behavior from which [fortunately] we are exempt. . . . *Our* god, by contrast—reason, science, criticism, the Logos, the spirit of human language and civilized conversation—is invisible, dynamic, and incapable of being reified in any material, spatial image.[6]

In contrast to the irrational persons who involve themselves in painting—pagans, primitives, children, foolish women, and Papists—wiser persons live by the creed of reason, science, and civilized conversation.

One of my reasons for researching this book was to discover the intellectual premises of those many I have encountered who are skeptical about the use of visual images in preaching. Frankly, this quote from Mitchell sets forth a clear answer to my search. Is it any wonder that the kind of people Lessing describes as "poetry-people" are opposed to "painting" in the preaching life of the church? We certainly can't have pagans and primitives and children and foolish women come to life and expression in the church. Mitchell's book showed me that my task in this book would be far larger than I had imagined. To Mitchell's way of thinking, the whole of the Western intellectual world can easily dismiss any arguments for the use of visual images in preaching. This chapter will propose an alternative to the dualistic thought of the Western intellectual enterprise.

Birth of the Western Intellectual Heritage

In the fourth century B.C.E., Plato and his younger contemporary Aristotle were engaged in thinking and debates that have profoundly shaped the history of Western thought. The intellectual problem of their day was the loss of absolutes, the loss of objective norms for determining what reality was all about. The highest value that had been proposed to fill this loss was individual self-interest; every individual must determine for him- or herself what is true, right, and beautiful.

Plato could not accept self-interest as the normative reality of life. For his alternative, Plato drew upon dualism. (No surprise there!) One world he identified is the world of the senses as perceived by sight, sound, touch, taste, and smell. The outstanding feature of the world experienced by the senses is that it is unstable, always changing. The other world, contrary to the world of sensate experience, is the realm of "forms" or "ideas." This world is fixed and changeless, so it is truly real. According to Edwin Burtt's summary of Plato's thought:

> the forms . . . are sharply distinguished from the transitory things of sense which in contrast with them become mere phenomena—that is, appearances of reality empty of substance and with no power of self-maintenance. The forms are not revealed to sense perception. . . . They are visible only to the

inward eye of reason, which is the faculty capable of grasping the changeless.[7]

In other words, we cannot perceive ultimate reality with our senses, because they are subject to constant change. Apprehension of the true reality can be achieved only through the inner eye of the soul, through the faculty of reason. This dualistic approach to eternal reality is precisely the dualistic approach outlined by Mitchell at the beginning of this chapter: distrust of human senses, superiority of mind over body, and superiority of internal thought processes over external relations to the sensate world. Ear is superior to eye, and so forth.

Plato was expressly critical of the whole world of culture and the arts. Jeremy Begbie writes that Plato interpreted the Prometheus myth as humans stealing the capacity for culture, "skill in arts," from the gods. This interpretation provides a context for understanding Plato's view of artistic endeavors. If the artist is using a stolen skill ("the proper prerogative . . . of the gods"), then we who enjoy the art "are technically receivers of stolen goods passed on to us by the various 'fences' who paint, write, compose, sculpt or whatever. . . . Art . . . is inherently transgressive of the limits which creation sets, and thereby constitutes an offence to the divine creativity which it emulates."[8]

Plato's critique of human culture is not surprising, considering that culture deals with matters of our senses. The world of the senses is the world humans need to escape in order to come to grips with the real worlds of "forms" and "ideas." Begbie explains Plato's view that artistic expressions move us away from truth; they "take us yet one step further away from truth, since a copy of a copy is bound to be paler and less adequate than the original copy; and the world, we must remember, is itself already a pale copy of the truth of things."[9] And Begbie associates this business of copying truth with the chief worry of iconoclasts: "Plato has no qualms about associating imaginative creativity with the human propensity to produce idols."[10] False gods. False reality represented as true reality. For Plato, as for Christian iconoclasts of every age, iconoclasm rests on a dualistic understanding of reality.

Aristotle differs markedly from Plato in his understanding of reality, notes Burtt. His main interests were scientific, not moral or religious. Aristotle used the scientific method to account for all the amazing realities of the sensate world. For Aristotle, the world of sense experience is not to be demeaned. The sensate world is the real world.[11] Forms are embedded in the objects we experience with our senses. Our knowledge of the real comes from reflection on our sense perceptions. The true nature of reality is induced by scientific investigation, not deduced by human reason from eternal "forms" and "ideas."

Aristotle is no dualist. He affirms the created world and considers sight the most important of the senses. Thomas Aquinas, who helped to introduce the philosophy of Aristotle to the medieval theological and philosophical world, writes in the *Summa Theologica* that sight takes place without any natural change in the organ or the object. Sight, therefore, is the most spiritual and most perfect of the senses. In the reflections of Aquinas, hearing takes second place behind seeing.

Thomas Aquinas, of course, had an enormous impact on medieval theology. He brought the thought world of Aristotle into theological play. As he evaluated seeing and the senses as "very good," we should not be surprised that the medieval church made such a strong appeal to the sense of sight through its images, icons, statues, paintings, and so forth. In time, as we saw in chapter 2, this visual presentation of the Christian faith dominated over the sense of the ear, hearing, until corrections came from both the Roman Catholic and "Reformed" Protestant worlds of thought.

In the Western Enlightenment project, the dualistic thinking we have observed in Plato and others was again at work. Like Plato, René Descartes responded to a sense of uncertainty regarding knowledge and the world. Descartes found the ground of certainty within his own mind: "I think, therefore I am." The intelligible world of ideas can be known by the mind, and the physical world is known through the senses, leaving an unbridgeable gap between those two worlds. Descartes thus underscored the skepticism regarding the ability of our senses to connect us to reality. His work helped make such skepticism a major fact of philosophical thought in the modern Western world. Dualism has reigned.

An incarnate God, a circumscribable God, elevates matter and the senses and thus opposes philosophical dualism. With such a God, the relation of humans to the ultimate reality, to the divine, is not just a relationship that exists in a spiritual moment of bliss of some kind. Our relationship to ultimate reality is also grounded in the material world that God blessed in creation and sanctified in the incarnation. One can make an image of this incarnate God. Images, in a sense, protect us from dualism by forcing us to deal with the sensory world. There is no unbridgeable gap between the world of the senses and the world of the mind; in fact, the world of the senses, in which God became incarnate, must be deeply involved in our process of thinking about reality.

Which is more important: painting or poetry, image or word, seeing or hearing? In the world of Western intellectual thought, as in the Christian church, this debate has reverberated through the ages, beginning with Plato and Aristotle. As I noted earlier, William Dyrness writes that the Platonic school of thought has held the upper hand in this debate, a dominance that has influenced the church as well: "Because of our Platonic heritage, we [the Christian community] privilege the invisible [and cognitive] over the visible, or to put it another way; we privilege meaning over form. But this is precisely what the Christian doctrines of creation and incarnation should make impossible."[12]

Who Killed the Goddess?

The conflict between word and image is often cast as a conflict between masculine (word) and feminine (images). In a provocative if speculative book, *The Alphabet versus the Goddess*, Leonard Schlain tackles this matter directly. Schlain is a professor of surgery at a medical school, and as a vascular surgeon, he has firsthand knowledge of the profoundly different functions performed by each of the brain's hemispheres. "My unique perspective," he writes, "led me to propose a neuroanatomical hypothesis why goddesses and priestesses disappeared from western religions."[13]

Schlain's interest in this topic arose from his observation that much evidence from the third millennium B.C.E. indicates that goddesses were the central focus of worship. His hypothesis on this matter links the decline of goddess worship to brain anatomy and physiology: "When a critical mass of people within a society acquire literacy, especially alphabet literacy, left hemispheric modes of thought are reinforced at the expense of right hemispheric ones, which manifest as a decline in the status of images, women's rights, and goddess worship."[14]

Schlain ranges over an amazing breadth of cultural information in coming to his conclusions. I am as impressed with the breadth of his knowledge as I am skeptical of some of his conclusions. He is convinced, for example, that writing subliminally fosters a patriarchal outlook in its linear massage of the human brain. "I propose that a *holistic, simultaneous, synthetic,* and *concrete* view of the world are the essential characteristics of a feminine outlook; *linear, sequential, reductionist,* and *abstract* thinking defines the masculine."[15] In Schlain's hypothesis, each person's worldview combines these two ways of thinking, which he associates with right-brain and left-brain dominance. Neither outlook is superior to the other; rather, these two sides of human possibility are complementary, not necessarily in contradiction, as in the Asian concept of yin and yang. On this foundation, Schlain makes his basic point:

> Goddess worship, feminine values, and women's power depend on the ubiquity of the image. God worship, masculine values, and men's domination of women are bound to the written word. Word and image, like masculine and feminine, are complementary opposites. Whenever a culture elevates the written word at the expense of the image, patriarchy dominates. When the importance of the image supersedes the written word, feminine values and egalitarianism flourish.[16]

Schlain is now ready to tell us who killed the goddess. The culprit, he says, was the development of alphabetic literacy: "First writing, and then its more sophisticated refinement, the alphabet, tolled the death knell of feminine values both metaphorically and, as we shall see, quite literally."[17] It was the Hebrews, he believes, who first founded a religion of words and book, the Torah. Schlain believes that the Old Testament was the first alphabetic written work to influence future ages! Along with the new religion of literacy and the book came a prohibition of all images, especially all images of the gods. Schlain believes that the Hebrew culture was the first culture in the world to forbid representative art. Now, with the writing of the Torah, the goddess was dead!

This killing of the goddess occurs, he points out, in all the major religions of the book: Judaism, Christianity, and Islam. (Yet recall from chapter 2 that John of Damascus maintained that because of the incarnation, the God of the Christian is circumscribable. It is possible to have images of an incarnate God but not to have images of an idea. These are the first religions based on abstract ideas and codified in books. And, he claims, they are also the first religions to go to war. People have been killed in wars because they believed in different abstract ideas. This thought is consistent with an idea we will discuss later: words are exclusive. People can be excommunicated, even killed, for not believing in the right words.

Without doubt, Schlain's conclusions are conjectures. His book intrigues me, however, because the alignment of masculine/word versus feminine/image is rife throughout the literature on the worth assigned to words and images. It is common to identify words with masculine/mind and images with feminine/body. In weighing these against each other, the males—who have generally given us our cultural arbitrations—have almost always preferred masculine values to feminine values. Somewhere at the heart of the conflict between words and images, there surely lies a dualism that pits the one against the other: the spiritual against the body, the infinite against the finite, the masculine against the feminine, and the word against the image. Schlain has tried to argue that these two worlds ought to exist as complementary, rather than as opposing worlds of insight. I agree. We must see word and image as complementary modes of thought if we are to recapture the sense of the visual in our Christian life and especially in our preaching.

Words and Images: Complementary Tools

Studying history from a fresh perspective, Margaret Miles searches for the ideas of *non–language experts*, often seen in the culture's visual components. The keepers of a culture's visual components, she asserts, are generally female. The artistic vision of cultures can therefore show us the often-neglected thought of the feminine world. While Miles specifically does not treat images as "the key" to understanding history, she calls them "a significant piece of the discourse of Christian communities, that has not been systematically incorporated in the study of historical Christian ideas," and she adds that studying images can change "our understanding of the whole discourse."[18]

Her comments here are very suggestive. I was trained as a systematic theologian. I worked with abstract ideas. I was never taught to think that the art of a given era—the Reformation era, for example—might give complementary and supplementary insights into the world of ideas of that time. If I understand Miles correctly, she is pressing people like me, trained theologians, to widen our perspective by giving attention to the visual culture that accompanied the works of the written culture. I don't think I could ever teach systematic theology again without giving much more attention to visual images as a source of theology.

It is interesting that the present world, which has been labeled postmodern, is far more open to a pluralism of resources for thought. Images are polyvalent. The truth gained from them is subjective. This fits the postmodern concept of the subjectivity of meaning. Ideas, however, assert a singularity of meaning. Truth is objective. I don't think we need to choose between the option of image/subjective and word/objective. Neither does Miles. Complementarity is again the order of the new day.

Miles intends to show that the kind of "subjective consciousness" associated with the word and abstract thinking is not the only way to deal with meaning:

> If the texts for the educated provide a history of the antecedents of the modern subjective consciousness, visual images provide a history of the way by which the nonprivileged understood and coped with physical existence. Only by attention to visual evidence can we begin to reconstruct a history of people [nearly all women] who identified themselves primarily with physical existence. It was to reveal and interpret the universality of physical existence that visual images existed; this was the reason for their ubiquity and popularity.[19]

A study of the images created in past cultures can help us discover forgotten, and often feminine, aspects of the total world of human thought that has preceded us.

Miles argues very persuasively that images must again stand in some kind of equivalence to ideas. She knows the ambivalence given to image in the Christian tradition and the problem of idolatry and superstition connected with the image. But although the church has fought against these problems, Miles writes, "None of the texts that caution against illegitimate attachment to images urges the rejection of all images. Rather, these texts indicate an awareness that a powerful tool is always double-edged, capable equally of providing valuable help and of promoting addiction to the tool itself."[20]

This is a crucial insight for our project. Either images or words used in isolation from the other can be addictive! Images crowd out meaning, or words crowd out imagination. We will want to hold the realities of images and words in equipoise.

In her book's last chapter, Miles sets forth a theory as to how words and images might best fulfill their proper role. Concerning the proper function of images in the life of Christians, she asserts:

> The image awakened and focused the worshiper's desire to imitate the spiritual characteristics presented by images. . . . It was not, however, the idea of transcendent spiritual qualities that attracted the worshiper to imitation of the image. Rather, the endurance, ecstasy, faith, or whatever spiritual quality was embodied by the image came to the worshiper not as an idea but as the embodied experience of a historical person. The image posited the possibility and the fruitfulness, *for embodied human beings,* of the depicted spiritual qualities.[21]

Human beings are incarnate, and Jesus Christ became incarnate in just such a body in order to redeem the human condition. The incarnation illuminates the usage of images and icons in Miles's understanding and is the same argument that John of Damascus used in the Eastern church's iconoclastic controversies. An embodied God in Christ for embodied humans can be represented in image and icon.

Miles then addresses issues that arise because images are adaptable to a variety of interpretations by a diversity of individuals. "As long as images played a prominent role in Christian worship, a wide variety of individual interpretations not only was tolerated by necessity but was accepted in Christian communities."[22] Hence language becomes necessary in its primary role as therapeutic or remedial. Language seeks to correct or balance otherwise destructive tendencies to spin meaning in all directions. Language helps to give definition to the spiritual experience of an icon/image. But the balance in the opposite direction has been less reliable:

> Western Christianity has been much more aware of image abuse than of language abuse, perhaps because language users were quick to detect and condemn exclusive devotional attention to images. Thus, careful rationales and guidelines for the use of images were . . . formulated and reiterated. Language users were not, however, so adept at self-criticism; compulsive concentration on religious language—language abuse—has not received much attention in western Christianity.[23]

Whereas theologians through the ages have been adept at using language to clarify theological ideas and make precise theological definitions, the words and language of theology often have totally excluded alternative understandings. Those with alternative understandings are excluded from the community, excommunicated, pronounced heretic, and sometimes killed. If images are *inclusive* and allow for a variety of interpretations, words can be *exclusive,* disallowing alternative interpretations. Non–language users, Miles notes, were often totally bewildered by the exclusive character of theological doctrine. Many of them coped by declaring, "I believe what the church believes." This was a non–language user's exasperated confession. No one was excluded who made such a confession![24]

Still, Miles appreciates that image users face their own temptations. In contrast to the language user's "preoccupation with precise statements and the universal enforcement of those statements," she writes, people who express themselves through images face the temptation of "diffusion, the tendency to neglect to understand and formulate the particular power of attraction the image has for the one who is drawn to it."[25]

The solution, according to Miles, is for image and word to live in creative tension with each other. Her insights here are seminal and convincing, offering preachers a theory we can use in properly assessing the role of words and images in our preaching. In arguing that "language and images need not compete," Miles lays out a role for each:

> Exaggerated claims for the capacity of either language or artistic images only prevent recognition of the proper bailiwick and particular effectiveness of each. Images are powerful, and the most powerful images accomplish with skill and economy what they do best: formation by attraction. Language is also

powerful; language is therapeutic; its role is to anticipate and to analyze misunderstandings of self and world.[26]

Miles notes that in the post-Reformation world, both Roman Catholic and Protestant churches accented word over image, poetry over painting. Because of this focus, the ancient function of images has often been neglected among us in the churches. This is a loss, because images draw the worshiper to imitate and participate in the qualities of life formulated by the image.

By neglecting images, Miles writes, the Christian community has neglected contemplation and failed to cultivate emotional engagement. She says, "Through the use of images, historical Christians were moved first to imitate and then to assimilate the strength, the courage, and the love they contemplated in religious art. . . . Religion needs images to accomplish its task of formation by attraction. . . . Religion without artistic images is qualitatively impoverished; art without religion is in danger of triviality, superficiality, or subservience to commercial or political interests."[27]

Although Miles is not addressing the specific topic of this book, the use of images *in preaching,* her argument for the complementary usage of poetry and painting is very helpful for thinking through this topic. As post-Reformation Christians, we have been shaped very much by a "word alone" mentality. But according to Miles, words alone simply will not do! This is true of our whole life of worship together, but it can also be true of our preaching. Words alone do not massage the entire human psyche. We also need images so we can more directly experience what the words denote. Words without images speak only to the left brain. Images without words speak only to the right brain. Words without images give us something to understand. Images without words give us something to contemplate. Words without images give us truth plainly. Images without words spark our religious imagination. Words need images. Images need words. This is a formula for fully orbed preaching.

An ancient Chinese saying effectively captures the complementarity of poetry and painting: "In every poem there is a picture; in every picture there is a poem." This saying comes to us out of a culture that values both/and formulations rather than the either/or formulations of the Western intellectual tradition. Another ancient Chinese saying also is appropriate for our study: "One hundred words for hearing are not as powerful as one image for seeing." Preaching can be understood as both/and with respect to poetry and painting, not either/or. Why, after all, preach to half a person?

William Dyrness, like Miles, pleads for a recapturing of the visual sense in theology and worship:

> Christians should not play the visual against the verbal. . . . [The visible forms of Christian art and architecture] some-times provided a more striking interpretation of Scripture than the texts of theologians—they were certainly more acces-sible to people. Indeed, these "media" were only rarely, during Christianity's iconoclastic periods, seen as being in competi-tion with each other. They were rather seen as complementary. Why can we not recover this wholesome synergy?[28]

Why not indeed? If we in the church do not provide images to com-plement our ideas, the secular world is waiting just outside the door to offer us its images for life.

Words and the Word Incarnate

If we will argue that Christians should not play the visual against the verbal, painting against poetry, images against words, we will move in the face of a strong Protestant prejudice for the word that comes to us from some of our Reformers. John Calvin is usually credited with being the father of this particular emphasis on words over images. As we reviewed in chapter 2, Calvin saw learning from images as futile and false; "pure preaching" was for Calvin the only proper and direct route to faith.[29] Calvin's teaching that images are idolatrous and detrimental to one's faith is a powerful legacy to the Protestant churches of this age. It is the reason much Protestant worship and preaching have been largely devoid of image. We are a church of the Word, and by *Word*, we usually mean the Bible. The Bible outlaws images. End of argument.

Protestantism is in many of its streams solely a religion of word; in fact, for many of us, even the meaning of *word* has been narrowed. *Word* has for many Christians become synonymous with *written word*. We can find an explanation in church history. Luther had a tool of reformation that no reformer before him had possessed: the printing press. I sometimes like to say that the Lutheran Church is the first church in the history of the world to be helped to its birth by the mass media—the mass media of the printed word. The development of the printing press and the Protestant discovery of "Word alone" (one of Luther's watchwords) go hand in hand. The Reformation sought to redress the conditions of the late medieval church, where the visual sense dominated the auditory sense. "Word alone" in the "book alone" got the job done quite well. It is almost inconceivable to imagine the Reformation even happening apart from the tool of the printing press. Protestantism and print, as many have shown, go hand in hand. We are dominantly churches of the Word. Preaching and teaching the Word is a basic mode of operation.

This Protestant formula has some distinct problems if and when "Word alone" means "Bible alone." In the first place, the Bible itself seeks to inform us that God's Word was an *oral* word long before it became a written word. The Bible opens with a literary testimony to the creative power of God's word of address: "Let there be light," *God said*, and there was light (Genesis 1). God speaks, and it is so. The prophet Isaiah (Isaiah 55:10–11) gives us a beautiful poetic description of the creative power of God's word of address:

> For as the rain and the snow come down from heaven,
>   and do not return there until they have watered the earth,
> making it bring forth and sprout, giving seed to the sower
>   and bread to the eater,
> *so shall my word be that goes out from my mouth;*
>   it shall not return to me empty,
> *but it shall accomplish that which I purpose,*
>   and succeed in the thing for which I sent it. (italics added)

Throughout the Old Testament, God spoke creative words of promise to Abraham and David and others, and God's word gave birth to what was promised. Abraham possessed the land and founded a people. David's reign became an eternal reign through the instrumentality of the Son of David, Jesus the Messiah (Christ).

The literary words of the New Testament, in turn, bear testimony that God's Word became incarnate in the person of Jesus Christ. God's Word made flesh spoke with the creative power of God. He spoke words of healing to the blind, and the blind could see. He spoke words of healing to the deaf, and they could hear. He spoke words of resurrection to the dead, and the dead became alive again. The Incarnate Word of God spoke, and his word created life: "In him was life, and the life was the light of all people" (John 1:4).

When we speak of the Word of God, therefore, we are speaking primarily of the oral word of God, secondly of this Word made flesh, and thirdly of a written record that bears witness to the salvation wrought through the oral and incarnate word of God. Martin Luther was very clear on this matter. He did not confuse "Word of God" with a book, the Bible:

> And the gospel should not really be something written, but a spoken word which brought forth the scriptures, as Christ himself did not write anything but only spoke. He called his teaching not scripture but gospel, meaning good news or a proclamation that is spread not by pen but by word of mouth. So we go on and make the gospel into a law book, a teaching of commandments, changing Christ into a Moses, the One who would help us into simply an instructor.[30]

Clearly, Luther thought of God's Word as an oral word of proclamation and address. The need to put the Gospels in writing, Luther thought, reflected a quenching of the Spirit. Life comes not from words in a book, but from the spoken word of God, whether that speaking is done by the Creator God, by God's Word Incarnate, or by preachers (and others) who address the promises of God as living promises to the faithful.

The written word of God is certainly central to the life and faith of Christian people. Let us not forget, however, that the creative oral word of God precedes the Bible. The written words of the Bible are to point us to the oral word of God, especially to the oral Word of God incarnate in Jesus. This, too, was clear for Luther. He understood the Bible to be a witness that points us to Christ. We need to be careful, therefore, in the ways we magnify the written word. Written words have often been held up as superior to painted words, but when we privilege the written word, we can all too easily identify Christianity as primarily a religion of the book. The strengths and weaknesses of the world of print then attach themselves to Christian perception.

A second problem of identifying our book as the heart of who we are is that it promotes dogmatic thinking that excludes others. For the monotheisms of the book, like Judaism and Islam, revelation is tied directly to writing, to the book. These faiths say, "God wrote a book for us!" Salvation is open to all who read the book, hear the book, and obey the book. Religions so designed often go to war to fight for the uniqueness and absoluteness of their ideas. Religions so designed often exclude those who read their book in other than their orthodox way. Religions so designed are tied to the absolute authority of their book. Religions so designed prohibit images. Religions so designed often see God solely as masculine. Religions so designed often denigrate the status of women.

But Christianity is not one such religion! God did not become a book or write a book for our salvation. We are not a religion dependent on a book for our salvation. Rather, God's Word became incarnate in the flesh. Our salvation depends on the creative Word of God make flesh for us in Jesus Christ. God became flesh, not a book! Our book bears witness to this salvation. Our words, including our preached words, bear witness to God's saving purposes. Our art also bears witness to our salvation. Our icons and images bear witness to our salvation. God created us as whole persons, and God encountered us in Jesus Christ as a whole person. God is not a kind of literate being off somewhere who decided to send us a love letter. God's love letter was etched upon the cross on which God died for us in Jesus Christ. God's offer of salvation is body for body, God's body for our body. It is not mind to mind.

As we learned from the iconoclastic controversies, this God of ours is circumscribable. You can see and smell and touch and feel and hear this God: "We declare to you what was from the beginning, what we have heard, what we have seen with our eyes, what we have looked at and touched with our hands, concerning the word of life" (1 John 1:2). You can paint pictures of this God. You can create icons. You can use visual images in preaching. We need to utilize all the senses to proclaim Jesus Christ to sensate beings. You can't make images of ideas in a book. You can make images of a God incarnate in the flesh.

The way we think of words, books, and Word of God has powerful implications for the content and nature of our preaching. If our entire focus for "Word of God" is a literate book, then preaching will naturally be given over to explaining and teaching the words of this book. Preaching will be primarily didactic. Faith will arise as those who hear our preaching understand and believe in the words of the Bible and do them. As I noted in the discussion of theosis in preaching in chapter 2, this focus separates the divine initiating activity of God and the responsive activity of the believer. But as Luther noted, when the person of Christ and that of the believer are separated in this way, salvation is still under the realm of the law: "If you divide Christ's person from your own," Luther said, "you are in the Law." You are under the written word that kills, not under the Spirit's life-giving word.

Preaching will take a different turn if we begin our deliberations about the content and nature based on the oral Word spoken by God, incarnate in Jesus. This is the Word we preach! We speak again to people the dynamic, life-giving Word of God. Preaching does what it says. God's word uttered through the mouth of the preacher is an instrument of the life-giving Spirit. That's what we said about theosis and preaching. Preaching mediates God's indwelling in the believer. Preaching is an instrument for divinization of the believer. Preaching mediates the transformation of human agency. Preaching mediates a union with Christ. Preaching mediates filling our lives with God. These are the kind of words we use to describe preaching as an oral event. Preaching, that is, lives in continuation with God's word that created life and God's Word Incarnate who offers life for the world today. Preaching, I believe, should take its cue from the oral character of God's word. Preaching is engaged in the task of *mediating* salvation to humans, not the task of *explaining* salvation to humans.

Preaching based on God's-word-as-book may find numerous reasons for excluding the use of images in preaching or worship. After all, that's what the book says in the second commandment, and book religions have always prohibited images. Christianity, however, is not a book religion, but a religion centered in an incarnate Word of God. This Word can be imaged. This Word can be circumscribed. Preaching can welcome the use of complementary visual images, which help people experience what our words proclaim. Images can be used to help with meditation and contemplation on the reality of our circumscribable God. Preaching can use poetry and painting to mediate a human experience of the reality and power of God's promissory word.

Returning to my basic point, words and images need each other. They are complementary, not contradictory. Each appeals to a facet of the human psyche. As W. J. T. Mitchell points out, there is no essential difference between poetry and painting that is inherent in the nature of the media or the laws of the human mind. There are differences of effect.

Miles, too, is helpful in noting the *exclusive* nature of words and the *inclusive* nature of images. Words can exclude. This is particularly true in our churches when our theological formulas, those we love and cherish, become idols. Someone who ceases to believe in the formulary of words of any denomination can be excluded from that community. Words then become anything but gospel, no matter how cherished the theological formula. Words become idols that we "worship."

This is hard for a trained theologian to confess! I love the Lutheran theological formulations. I think they are wonderful, right, and true. I have taught them, and I continue to teach them. But I have learned over time, particularly in the process of thinking through the relationship between word and image, that I dare not make an idol of these words. These words and formulas are not truth incarnate. They point to the truth incarnate. Augustine is reported to have once said that the words in our creeds are not truth in themselves. They are more like stop signs on the road to heresy. Full truth, complete truth, is always much larger than any words we might use to encapsulate truth. When our formulas claim to be the be-all and end-all of truth, they are in grave danger of becoming idolatrous. Words need images to prevent them from this fate. Words need images to give us more than one medium through which to experience the truth of God's promissory word.

Images, as Miles has taught us, are inclusive because they are polyvalent, open to many interpretations. One can meditate on an image of the prodigal son and experience a variety of realities as the story speaks to our unique situation in life. The hope is, of course, that some people will be grasped by God's word of grace more clearly through the image of the prodigal son than by the words of our sermon, which point out the meaning of the parable and align that meaning with denominational theology. People "see" things differently through an image. In fact, the image often communicates when the word does not, communicating to some people far better than words. But there is a problem here as well. The image can become so diffuse in meaning that it means literally anything or nothing, or its meaning to a given individual can move far beyond the bounds of the church's teaching. So, images *need* words to give them meaning, boundary, and definition.

Other writers have expressed similar roles for art. Janet R. Walton, in *Art and Worship: A Vital Connection*, describes the inclusive character of an artist's work:

> Artists work intensely in non-discursive forms that proceed from intuition rather than well-tested facts. While they use patterns of logic to express relationships, they do not necessarily follow literal, linear patterns but rather the logic of symbolic forms. In other words, they offer vehicles of conception that contain meaning rather than proof to substantiate it. The interpretation is left to the participant.[31]

Andrey Tarkovsky, the great Russian film artist of the twentieth century, applies similar thinking to the art of filmmaking. He believes that through an image an awareness of the infinite, the eternal within the finite, occurs:

> The allotted function of art is not, as we often assume, to put ideas across, to propagate thoughts, to serve as example. The aim of art is to prepare a person for death, to plough and harrow his soul, rendering it capable of turning to good.

Gogol wrote to Zhukovsky in January 1848: "It is not my job to preach a sermon. *Art is anyhow a homily.* My job is to speak in *living images,* not in arguments. I must exhibit *life* full-face, not discuss life."[32]

Preaching cannot be satisfied with simply *discussing* the life that is ours in Jesus the Incarnate One. Preaching, too, must exhibit life "full-face" so that those who hear do experience and participate in God's good news.

Given the idea that words and images are conceived differently toward different ends, preaching needs them both in order to reach the hearts of all the faithful. Preaching needs the full scope of words and images because our congregants need a variety of avenues to understand and experience the truth of God's promise. Preaching needs the full scope of words and images because our congregants learn in a variety of ways. Preaching needs the full scope of words and images because people are different and we, like Paul, are determined as preachers to "become all things to all people, that [we] might by all means save some," doing so "for the sake of the gospel" (1 Corinthians 9:22–23).

I spoke once with a male pastor of a large urban congregation that had a church facility well wired for visual presentations. I asked him if he used the screens in his preaching. He replied, "Yes, we do. I use it to put up the outline of my sermon. My female assistant uses it to put up images of her sermon." Who is right here—the male with his words or the female with her images? That's the wrong question. We need them both!

Pierre Babin, in a 1991 book titled *The New Era in Religious Communication,* notes that up until the time of the printing press, all instruction in the church was right-brain instruction.[33] Teaching took place through images, icons, morality plays, and the "Bible in picture," which filled the churches. After the creation of the printing press, all instruction in the church became left-brain book learning. Babin's plea was that in this "new era in religious communication," we need a *stereo catechesis.* Teaching and learning need to be targeted to the full human sensorium. This is good advice for preaching as well. We need *stereo* homiletics! We need outlines *and* pictures. We need words *and* images. We need poetry *and* painting.

Our journey through the rise of art in the early church, the dominance of the visual on the eve of the Reformation, the iconoclastic controversies, and Western philosophy's debate over the relative merits of poetry and painting provides ample evidence to justify the use of visual images in our preaching. Thinking in picture as a way of preaching is grounded in the history of the use of art in the church's life. Visualizing the Word of God is an ancient discipline in the life of the church that can help us reach people today. Thinking in picture is grounded in a theology of creation and incarnation, including the idea that the finite can communicate the infinite. Thinking in picture in our preaching also can help us engage the imagination of those who "see" the sermon. Because of the sensory impact (words for ears, pictures for eyes), our preaching might also hold the congregation's attention as our message embeds itself more deeply in human memory. Furthermore, as Margaret Miles writes, neglect of image is neglect of contemplation. Contemplation is a healthy response to sermons that are seen as well as heard. Miles adds that the need for images extends to formation of the Christian life because images attract and engage us in their reality. Finally, thinking in picture is an important aspect of preaching because our culture is highly visual.

Appealing to the Religious Imagination

Robert Wuthnow, a distinguished figure in the world of sociological studies of religion in the United States, recently published a book that seeks to explain why the religious vitality of American life hardly diminished in the last fifty years. In spite of seeming evidence to the contrary, what particularly strikes Wuthnow about American religion in the last decades of the twentieth century is how remarkably stable it was. He mentions three major explanations that have been offered—growth in conservative churches, entrepreneurial church leadership that revitalizes congregations, and strength in groups who fight for their rights as an embattled subculture in the society—but provides sociological data contradicting the importance of each explanation.

What then is the answer? Wuthnow's conclusion surprised him and surprises many others: "*One of the most important reasons that spirituality seems so pervasive in American culture is the publicity it receives because of its presence in the arts. . . .* My interviews with rank-and-file Americans suggest that many have been prompted to think about spirituality by participating in the arts or by being exposed to the arts as consumers."[34] He notes that this is true both of secular culture, which often deals with religious themes, and of the churches' culture, in which music and art are dominant. In interviews, people told Wuthnow of various kinds of exposure to art and music:

> Many have vivid memories of Bibles, wall hangings, crucifixes, and other sacred objects in their homes. . . . The childhood exposure that matters most is not attendance at services but the subliminal contact with the holy that comes through hymns and other religious music, pictures, Bibles, crosses, candles, and other sacred objects.[35]

Citing statistical chart after statistical chart, Wuthnow concludes that the arts *may be* a source of vitality for our religious institutions. This would be true, he writes, for a significant minority of the population—perhaps a quarter of the public—who appear to be serious about their spiritual growth. This quarter of the populace, writes Wuthnow, is the main source of the grassroots vitality in the nation's churches and synagogues. This leads Wuthnow to propose that in the future, religious revitalization may come from use of the arts. Wuthnow offers some recommendations:

> Religious organizations must channel these [artistic] interests in ways that encourage serious commitment to spiritual growth, and, in turn, involvement in congregations. . . . The lion's share has to be done through congregations, small groups, retreat centers, publishing efforts, and other vehicles by which the public comes into contact with organized religion. . . . [Existing efforts] range from contemporary worship services and liturgical renewal efforts in congregations to small group ministries and spiritual direction programs, to artistic initiatives aimed at encouraging the religious imagination, to cooperative ventures between community arts organizations and churches.[36]

Wuthnow's advice calls upon our ability to reach the religious imagination. His suggestions open many doors and windows for church outreach. To reach the imagination, art and music are two vital tools. How might we best use them? How can we cooperate with community arts organizations? What new strategies might we employ? A congregation in Prospect Heights, Illinois, has a strategy for the arts and has published a manual titled *The Arts Anew Manual*, available online at www.good-shep.org. Another tool— and the thrust of this book—is preaching accompanied by visual images. Wuthnow's study shows that people give overwhelming support to such communication through arts and music in the life of the church. As a practical example, Wuthnow offers an anecdote in which a woman convinces her husband to attend Willow Creek Community Church (South Barrington, Illinois) with her: "He had always taken an intellectual approach to religion, found himself unable to believe, and went knowing he wasn't going to learn anything from the preaching. But the multimedia presentation and the drama made an impact. 'The arts did an end run around the back and kind of nipped me, and I didn't realize it.'"[37] Wuthnow adds that the husband eventually became an active church leader.

I have a longtime friend who is now retired but serving with another pastor in a very small Lutheran congregation in Japan. My friend had been a seminary professor, worked on the Lutheran World Federation staff, and excelled as a college president. As soon as he took up his retirement call in the small parish, he explored ways that the congregation's outreach might appeal to the religious imagination. A member of his congregation, a highly successful photographer, provides a different photo each month to lead into their Web site. It is beautifully done. The church also frequently hosts concerts and drama for the whole community. Growth in Japanese congregations comes hard, but attendance has increased significantly through this congregation's outreach to the religious imagination. Why does it work? Wuthnow says it is because music and visual art are so important to spiritual life: "They draw people closer to God, often by expressing what cannot be put into words. They spark the religious imagination and enrich personal experiences of the sacred. . . . Especially for people who have grown weary of metaphysical arguments, the arts provide an attractive alternative."[38]

I began this study with the hope of providing an intelligent rationale for the use of visual images in preaching. One of my students, now a pastor in the Midwest, says no such rationale is needed for the laity. I do know from my own experience that opposition to images in preaching does exist. For that reason, I have offered three chapters of background in history, theology, and art in the church's life to buttress the case for a legitimate use of visualization in preaching.

This rationale for the use of visuals in the homiletical arts provides a foundation for part 2. In the next two chapters, we will look at the practical matters attending the use of visualization in preaching.

Part II

THE VISUALIZING PROCESS

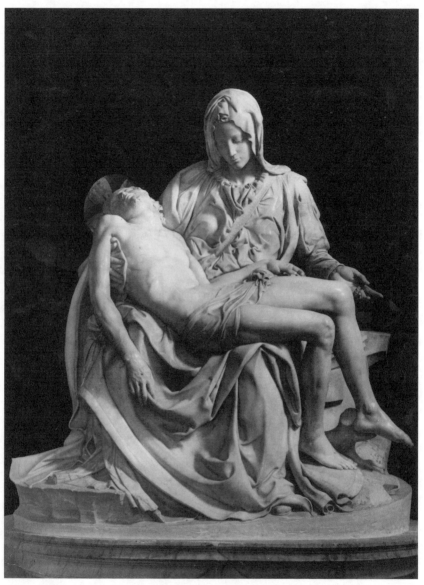

Michelangelo (1475–1564). *The Píeta.* St. Peter's Bascilica, Vatican, Rome. (Alinari/Art Resource, N.Y. Used by permission.) See pages 138 and 140.

4

Visualizing Salvation

BUILDING ON PART I's theological and theoretical arguments for using visual images in preaching, we turn now to practical matters. How do we preach with images? What equipment do we need? Do we work alone or through lay committees? Where do we find visuals? The questions are myriad. As I indicated in the introduction, the experts in this subject are the pastors actively engaged in using visual images in their preaching. Each of them has learned by trial and error. They are today our best teachers of how to "visualize salvation."

To learn from these experts, I interviewed a number of pastors in person and/or through a questionnaire. These pastors serve in small, medium-sized, and large churches in a variety of denominations. Some have more experience than others. Together they have a wealth of wisdom to share with us.

To present their insights and experiences, I have structured this chapter to follow the order of questions in the questionnaire. After restating each question, I summarize or quote (and sometimes comment on) what I have considered to be the best wisdom of these parish pastors on the visualizing process. The responses come from clergy who actively use visual images in their preaching. This method is neither exhaustive nor a scientific survey, but simply a report of what some pastors are doing, intended to help you in your own process of thinking in picture.

Getting Started

What were the factors that led you to decide to use pictures/visuals/ graphic images in your preaching?

As I got to know this new, younger community, I realized that popular music, TV, and movies were much more often on their lips than scripture quotations. I began to get ideas but was afraid to take big steps. Finally, in a leap of faith, I showed a movie clip from The Matrix *in a service. I could not have anticipated the impact this one sermon would have on the rest of my ministry.*

The positive response of the people overwhelmed this pastor. He added, "I had discovered the language of my culture."

It was a combination of experiences in my seminary teaching parish, in the classroom at seminary, and from various conferences I attended. An exploration into what it means to be Christian in a postmodern age also led me to ask how we can make the experience of the sermon more relevant and indigenous to the experience of those in the pews. On a personal level, I came to the realization that I rarely sit and do one thing. I channel surf 200 channels on the TV while browsing the Internet and talking on the phone. If that is at all a common experience, how can we further engage our parishioners in our sermon on different levels at the same time . . . using all the senses?

Another pastor wrote that she has used pictures or graphics in preaching from the beginning of her ministry: "Pictures or images can depict the idea often better than all the words. The visual was often the key to help people remember the point of the sermon." Her first parish had no fancy equipment, so she used low-tech visuals. Let's not forget this possibility in all the talk of the marvelous and expensive equipment that is available for visualization. A picture in the bulletin, a visual object of some kind, a dramatization of a story, and many other simple possibilities exist for the visualization process.

I wouldn't say that I made a conscious and systematic decision to use visuals—but when I see a movie or an image that helps illustrate the Gospel lesson—then I use the image. . . . I'm not making an intentional effort to use visuals, but they occasionally make their way into my sermons just as a story or illustration from life would.

As we shall see, many pastors made a similar point. They noted over and over that one should not use visuals just for the sake of using visuals. Rather, the use of visualization should grow naturally out of text study and other preparation for the sermon.

One pastor wrote that he got interested in visualization after attending a symposium at a large church in Arizona. He believed what he saw there would be relevant "back home." He also notes that he is most fundamentally excited about the use of visualization as an evangelism tool. Indeed, many of the pastors indicate that people who are coming to the church for the first time are the most ardent supporters of visualization.

Another pastor talked primarily about her motivation for the use of visuals. She believes that visuals give people something they will remember. She is also aware that people have different learning styles that need to be appealed to. Visuals can transport people to a different time and place; they spark the imagination.

A pastor in a large congregation wrote that he was interested in making this move because he recognized that the visual sense is a vital component of learning and education. On the practical level, he realized that other congregations were using projection and visual images in worship very effectively. His congregation needed to renovate its worship space, which provided an opportunity to build in the necessary equipment. The members did so willingly because they wanted "to reach out with the Gospel with creativity and the best use of current technology." During the renovation, they discovered they could project their images on walls and had no need for screens. Decisions about where to project visuals are often a major hurdle, especially if the congregation has to decide where to put a screen in a building that was never built for such a possibility. There are a grand variety of solutions to this problem. Any method that has the approval of the majority of the congregation and that is tastefully done within the architectural realities of a given building is possible.

A pastor identified four factors that led him to decide to use visuals:

1. Benefits of multisensory learning
2. "Word made flesh"
3. Postmodern emphasis on the visual
4. Renewal of preaching

Another said he was influenced to begin a visualization process in preaching because he had used it in worship with very positive results. He discovered that people in our culture are accustomed to getting information from a screen. He believed the church should keep up with culture in its forms of communication. Fortunately, as he was going through this process himself, the time came for renovation of the church building. Installing a projection system during the renovation was simple.

How did you prepare your congregation for change?

One respondent prepared his congregation for change by first using visuals just to project the lyrics of hymns. Next he began to project outlines and main points of his sermons. He then began projecting the announcements for upcoming activities before the beginning of each service. Finally, he added PowerPoint presentation software to his sermon, with occasional use of video clips. He now uses PowerPoint every Sunday. As we will see, pastors differ widely in the frequency of their use of visual images in preaching.

According to one pastor, when he reported to his first call, he discovered that the congregation already had purchased much of the equipment but had never used it in connection with preaching. One Sunday he just decided to go ahead and try it. "Using my own laptop, I prepared a sermon using visuals, put up the screen prior to my sermon, and took it down after the sermon. I did not prepare them. The response was quite positive."

Another pastor fell into a windfall in her new congregation. The church building had just undergone a $2 million renovation that included the installation of $150,000 worth of equipment for visualization. Still, she began very simply, displaying a work of art that helped to visualize the text for the day. "They were able to see the piece of art as I talked about it. They experienced the value of the equipment. They now realize that multimedia can enhance their own worship."

A pastor said her congregation was going through this change at the time of her response: "The worship committee has agreed to the purchase of a[n] LCD projector and screen. Part of the education of the community will be in the newsletter and through sermons."

One pastor talks about starting the process with his congregation through a series of baby steps. Working with the worship committee, he gradually changed the worship materials used in the congregation. He used a single piece of art occasionally in his preaching. This resulted in meetings with the congregation's leaders. Their support for going ahead was based primarily on their interest in visualization as an evangelism tool.

In some contexts, it is obviously very important to lay a careful groundwork for this change. Another pastor prepared her congregation through temple talks and newsletter articles. She invited in a pastor skilled in visualization in the whole worship experience to conduct a service. It was highly publicized and well attended. Eventually, a proposal was made to the church council that it approve the use of visualization. The measure passed. The whole process took several months.

Yet another pastor listed several methods used for preparing the congregation for change:

- Incorporated video technology and equipment into strategic plan/assessment of ministry needs and into the capital campaign.
- Interpreted the value of visual projection/video technology for communication of the gospel.
- Encouraged awareness of what other congregations were accomplishing in this area.
- Gradually and selectively incorporated the use of video technology into the worship experience and life of the congregation.

Another respondent noted that he worked for six years with the congregation, seeking to move them from a membership congregation to a discipleship congregation. Through this process, the congregation became acclimated to a climate of change "for the sake of spreading and growing in the Good News." The visualization process itself went through many stages: First, the pastor talked with key leaders who understood and supported projection. He then met with the church council and the building committee. He wrote about projection several times in the church newsletter. He spoke briefly at the annual meeting to get approval for funding of the whole building project. "We never made a big deal out of projection," he writes. "We just made sure key people understood and supported it." This had to be followed up with the use of equipment that would "knock their socks off." After a first use, projection was not used again for two months. However, the equipment remained visible in the sanctuary, as if to say, "Get used to this stuff. It's here." Clearly, this process was well thought through and carefully laid out.

Getting Technical

Pastors responding to the questionnaire indicated that they use a variety of technical equipment. They emphasized the importance of having technology that is good enough so that it is not a barrier to the viewer. People in congregations are used to superb delivery of visual programming on television. They will notice if our technology is of markedly poorer quality. We need to be sure that the technology used will not be a barrier to our communication of the gospel.

What technical equipment do you use?

The answers to this question varied widely. It will not be helpful to list some of their descriptions of equipment because much of it is now outdated. One pastor wrote: "The technology will continue to evolve and change. I've been here just shy of three years and we've been changing constantly." He went on to make the point that the technology available for church use is ever evolving. Those persuing this matter on behalf of their congregation need to gather the best advice available to them in their community. One pastor told a story of a member who belonged to his congregation who owned an electronics supply store who gave the church recently outdated but very good equipment for their use. Most congregations have some "experts" in technology in their midst who will be pleased to share their wisdom.

One source that was consistently praised by the respondents was Fowler Productions, who specialize in assisting with these technical matters: 1-800-729-0163.

What did the equipment cost?

The question of equipment cost is another matter that changes rapidly. One pastor who began this process spending $10,000 thought he could have done it a few years later for $6,000. This price may be adequate only for the most minimal amount of equipment needed for projection purposes. An average for start-up costs may run from $6,000 to $20,000. Some congregations have spent much more than that. One reported spending $45,000, another $150,000.

These costs are subject to many variables—the nature of your building itself, the quality of the equipment purchased, the amount of equipment purchased, and so forth. Congregations will want to search their community well for the right equipment at the right price.

Have you made use of congregational members with technical expertise?

The predominant answer to this question is an emphatic yes. I'll never forget speaking at a pastors' conference hosted by a pastor who wanted to introduce multimedia ways to those in attendance. After I spoke, he led a multimedia worship and preaching experience. For the media work, he got one of his junior high girls excused from class to do the technical stuff for us. She was so very proud of her work.

One respondent to this question simply said, "Absolutely." An electrician in the congregation had installed the wiring for the screen. An audiovisual technician did the wiring for the projector, computer, DVD, and VCR. A computer salesman in the congregation gave them a good deal on their purchase of equipment. "For us this has been a very collaborative process."

All of our equipment was installed by a congregational member who teaches theater tech at a local college. He also is our main multimedia/ sound person. He has taught others in the congregation as well. Having a media guru is marvelous.

We have a volunteer who puts the material on-screen each week. She is more of a creative person than a technical person, but her knowledge of the equipment is sufficient for us.

We have two primary operators who have special expertise in this area of technology and were previously not involved in any aspect of ministry apart from worship. Our goal is to expand and develop this crew.

One pastor indicated that his congregation uses an A/V team of four members. "They are out there," he wrote of his congregation's technical talent. He added that young people can be an excellent help in this area.

A woman member of our congregation was extremely helpful in designing, setting up, training operators, and introducing projection to the congregation. She was simply invaluable to our process.

The overall advice seems to be to involve from the very beginning laity who have gifts in this area. Others can be trained to help. People who have never found how their skills mesh with congregational needs are often moved into active membership through their participation in the media ministry of a congregation.

Making It Happen

We come now to the heart of the matter. How do you move from text study to visual imagination? The pastors who responded to my questionnaire gave a variety of suggestions, which I hope will be helpful as you pursue this matter.

What is it in the exegetical process that moves you toward visualization?

One pastor in a very conservative setting has an elaborately devised scheme or "matrix," which he uses as a structure to work on his sermon each week. Preparation, he indicates, always begins with a scriptural text. After his initial work with the text, he meets with the congregation's worship-media team to discuss the text and to begin move toward the kind of multimedia elements that might be appropriate. "This is their world," he says. "They know far more than they think they know. I couldn't imagine working on a sermon alone anymore." He monitors the group to be assured that everything they do "is in service of communicating the text in a way that builds a new world in the minds and hearts of the listener, empowering them to live by faith in new ways." He adds, "Working together has changed the way we do church."

One of the keys that opened another pastor's eyes to hearing texts in new ways from the standpoint of the laity was his study of narrative criticism. Narrative criticism is a relatively new tool for studying the Bible. One of its central elements is that biblical texts have a *surplus* of meaning. Biblical texts speak differently to different readers/hearers. Hearing texts in new ways is often the key for his group in creating the images for preaching that open a new window on scripture.

Another clergyman works six months in advance to select the texts for the weeks to follow. Work on an individual sermon begins with biblical study and proceeds to a search in the text for images that might help to communicate the text. This is followed closely by an actual search for visuals in the image sources he is familiar with. This pastor does not work with a group in this process: "If we used a team, we would need to be at work on texts a month or so in advance of a given Sunday."

In preparing my sermons, I begin by memorizing the Gospel. This process allows me to visualize and get "inside" the text in a unique way. I visualize the parables, teachings, and accounts of any given text. In doing so, it informs what visuals I might choose to use—or not to use—in preaching.

Usually in my meditation and thought process, something will cross my mind that works well. Sometimes it comes from a resource, that suggests something that then stimulates an idea within me that comes from my own life experiences. I try and visualize the scripture. I think about how that might be put into today's context, and often from that process a movie will come to mind. Once in a while, if I haven't used a visual lately, I will go to a movie-art resource that is lectionary based to see if any of their suggestions click.

In the beginning, I used to do a great deal of work in commentaries, language study, etc. Now, I find myself looking through the lens of the Gospel, the cross, and applying that which I see in the movies, etc. To the cross and then into the lives of the people. I continue to read commentaries, but I'm more likely to focus on the writer's overall theme and then bring it to life through a novel or movie.

I tend to read the text and let it sink into the everyday fabric of my life. If an image comes to mind and it enhances the Gospel rather than getting in the way—then I use it. I guess that is to say that I don't try to think of a visual to go with the Gospel. I try to let it be a more organic process.

Visualization is the last thing I do. I only use it if it is the best way to communicate the text. The message comes first, visuals second. Grasping an image is like grasping an illustration. It should serve to help the congregation participate in the reality of the text. Participation is the key. You hope people experience the reality of the message.

Quite often the images just spring to mind—in fact, if I don't think of an image/film clip, etc., right away, I probably won't come up with one at all unless, of course, I get ideas from others in our weekly text study with pastors.

The incarnational dimension of the text . . . the desire to communicate the word that becomes flesh . . . the connection between faith in daily life. Out of study and reflection on the text, images bring the message and key themes into focus in ways that add or contribute to the experiential dimension of the Word.

When we are speaking about things that so often can be at best inadequately expressed with words, using additional forms of communication not only can help, but is finally essential. Jesus used "visuals," such as referring to the flowers and birds around him in the Sermon on the Mount. The church has always used visuals: paintings on church ceilings, stained glass windows, icons, statues, symbols made of shapes and colors. So projection is just doing the same old thing.

Finally, of course, the movement from text to visualization is a matter of individual gifts, taste, and intuition. Each of us will probably find different ways to set loose this creative process. One bit of helpful advice for all us of from the ideas respondents offered is the advice that images should not be forced. Scripture remains central. We use images not for entertainment purposes but to enhance the realities of the text for the lives of our hearers. It is the gospel that finally matters most, not our images. When words and images can work together effectively, however, we reach a wider range of the human sensorium. This possibility makes our work toward visualization vital for our preaching.

Do you sense a process at work that moves you toward visualization?
Respondents touched upon this issue in their earlier answers, but they had some helpful thoughts to add. They encouraged us to wake up our imagination. Many stated that working with a team is invaluable. Others prefer to do this creative process alone. The goal, wrote one, is to find an image that will reinforce or tie textual ideas to the realities of hearers' lives. Another said she does not really have such a process and instead relies on conversations with her staff and "aha" moments. One interesting comment comes from a pastor who says she "absolutely" has a process: "I seem to see in 3D these days."

Still another says, "The way I think and learn has always been by visualizing. If I read a text, I picture the scene. So, it is easy for me to use visuals. It seems like a natural extension of my style of communication." Scripture, of course, is the ground of the imagination in this process. Many indicate that it is simply in the process of text study that images arise. Prayer time also is important, say others. People who identify themselves as "visual learners" are particularly gifted in this area. They are also good mentors for others.

So far, I've noticed more that visualization moves me toward a different process when I prepare sermons. Knowing that projection is now a part of sermons forces me to think very differently about what I prepare. Especially at first, I had to think so hard that my head literally hurt in a good way while preparing sermons. It's very exciting to be forced to work with all the possibilities here. [It is hard work learning to think in a new way. It is hard work to learn to think in picture.] A process also moves me toward visualization. For example, some scriptural images are visual and cry out for a picture to go along with hearing them and hearing about them. The same is true about many life and world situations.

How do you use visuals in preaching?
The respondents gave interesting answers to this important question. Their responses are very helpful in guiding us into a new world of homiletical preparation.

I am very sensitive about what visuals I use so that I do not use anything that would offend either the adults or the children. Sometimes there is a film clip that works well and yet we have to advise people to view it critically. The things we show in the interplay of the elements (sight, sound, etc.) must keep everyone focused on the text of scripture. The images we show often give greater context and meaning to the text.

I use visuals in a rhetorical manner to help concretize points and make transitions. I use them also to inspire people. Some pictures really are worth a thousand words. I use them for the sake of illustration: from ear to eye to heart. I use them to convey humor, emotion, and dramatic tension. I also use them to legitimize an idea. People see that there is a reference point for my idea.

I generally do one of three things:

- *[I will] project one image that complements the message being shared. For example, a sermon dealing with 9/11 might have the picture of the two steel girders that were formed into a cross at Ground Zero.*
- *I will project many images that complement what I am saying. For example, a sermon on transformation might talk about how age inevitably transforms all people. I might rifle through many pictures of people starting as newborns until I am projecting people who are very old. I might finish off with a split picture of a newborn and someone who is very old, to highlight such transformation.*
- *I will project a movie clip as an illustration. Preachers often tell stories to illustrate the Gospel, so why not incorporate a movie clip. A sermon on sharing the Gospel might be complemented by the scene from Amistad where the slaves learn and share the Gospel through an illustrated Bible. A sermon on grace might be complemented by a scene from* Paying It Forward *where a guy crashes his car and someone comes out of nowhere and offers his brand-new Jaguar for free.*

Sometimes it is a concrete visual that the cameras can focus on. Sometimes it is a piece of art that I have up either through all of the sermon or just during the part where I refer to it. Sometimes it is a video clip that I lead into and then follow with some closure. The videos are often used as one of two or three sermon examples. This summer I did a series based on popular songs that people were given an opportunity to suggest. Some of the songs came from musicals and so the video of the song became the center of my sermon. There are times when the video clip has such an emotional impact, that I need to pause for it to sink in and then close with a closing word or sentence.

A couple of times I have shown clips from movies, but much of the time I bring a picture or paint a picture with words either describing a piece of art or a scene from a book. A lot of times people tell me they go home and look up the picture on the Internet.

I use film clips. Sometimes I just use an image on the screen during my sermon. With other sermons I might use something as simple as a sermon outline or bullet points.

A common suggestion is that film clips should be four to six minutes in length.

First of all, we have two projectors that project images underneath the arms of a huge cross in the chancel area. This gives us the capability of either projecting the same image on both sides or different images on each side.

- *To accent and develop theological themes. For example, in focusing on the* Communion of Saints and Baptism as a Lifelong Journey, *the right side image was an eighty-three-year-old beloved member whose memorial service we had celebrated the day before, and the left side images were of a baby being baptized that day together with the parents.*
- *As a focus for a time of reflection and prayer at the conclusion of the sermon. In a sermon titled "Living on Both Sides of the Rainbow," ten different images of rainbows were used together with Eva Cassidy's soulful rendition of "Somewhere over the Rainbow" as an invitation to prayer and reflection. The images and music followed the development of the rainbow promise from Genesis 9 together with Mark's account of Jesus' baptism and temptation in the wilderness.*
- *Occasionally using images throughout the sermon. Most often they are used during a portion of the sermon.*
- *To nurture relationships, community, and the experience of vicarious participation. Digital pictures from youth retreats have*

been projected as a way to connect with scripture and sermon themes. These images reveal/disclose the essence of a spiritual retreat that was otherwise invisible/unknown to the congregation. The result creates a new experience of community that is not possible to achieve with only an oral telling of the retreat story. At another level the youth, who are often invisible to the adult members of the congregation, become visible through the use of images in a way that enriches and deepens the definition of Christ's body. The use of images also is consistent with the experience of God's Word as surprise and new creation. What I am referring to are passages from Isaiah and elsewhere that refer to a new thing God is doing. Don't you see it? Look. Behold. The experience of discovery is how the Spirit works and how faith grows. The use of images can nurture this experience of discovery.

I project words to outline and/or emphasize key points. I use pictures or video [clips] that support and enhance key points. I need to learn much more.

How often do you make use of visual material in your preaching?

As you would expect, the answers to this question vary greatly. A strong theme, however, is that the visuals must grow out of the biblical text study. No one argues for visuals for visuals' sake.

I use visual material 80 percent of the time. It is mostly video clips.

Weekly. I use an occasional video or slide show.

Probably half of the time.

I do not use visuals every week. I like some variety. I only use a visual if it truly fits with the sermon. I'm not using something just because you are supposed to for a certain style of worship. One of my rules is, the visual has to be integrated into the sermon and add to the sermon or it will not be used. There are times when I thought I would use a visual, but it didn't quite take the sermon where I wanted and I discarded it.

In my current call, I am just beginning the process. I expect that I will use it at least once every six weeks at the beginning.

Maybe once a month.

I only use visuals when needed. I only use movie clips when it is impossible not to do so. To use visuals two weeks in a row in our parish would be a problem.

It depends on the text and my level of inspiration. Not as often as I'd like to.

Approximately two-thirds of the time. The other third images are used at some other time in the worship experience (prayer, gathering, sending, offering, etc.).

Every Sunday.

Do you work with a group of people in the planning process, or do you work alone?
The pastors responding to the questionnaire manage this process in different ways. Only a very few work alone. Most work with one or more groups in the process of creating the Sunday-morning total worship experience.

It is very important for me to work with laity in this process. I see this as a living example of the "priesthood of all believers." So, the first thing I did was to develop a team with a variety of people. They are experts in the culture and have excellent suggestions. Skilled or teachable laity are the key to a seamless multimedia experience. We call our group the "Worship Media Team." They both help to prepare the weekly experience and assist me in evaluating what we have done.

I design and produce. The AV team edits and executes the message.

I generally work alone, although there are some collaborative efforts from time to time. I also collaborate with colleagues.

I work with a small group every Monday to plan the Praise Worship, in which we talk about the sermon ideas and the music. Sometimes the visual idea comes from that part of the process.

In the initial stages, I'll work alone for the first time out. After that I hope to have a preaching team put together.

So far, mainly alone. But I've learned that I need more people in order to even come close to using the possibilities offered by projection. One of the necessary next steps for us is identifying and involving others in a way that is effective, doable, and sustainable.

I go to a text study—but the nitty-gritty is done on my own.

At this time the planning group consists of office and pastoral staff. Our goal is to develop a group that includes members/disciples whose gifts and passions would be a good fit in this area of ministry. The planning process begins with the pastoral staff in terms of worship/preaching themes and seasons. At this time the selection of specific images is done by the preacher for the day. After selecting images for a specific Sunday, I then e-mail them to our office administrator, who then puts them into a PowerPoint presentation. We then review and tweak the presentation, and I write instructions for the sound and video crew.

Alone or with our projectionist.

If you work in a group, how large is it and how are members chosen?
Again, the answers vary widely. Although it would be convenient if we would discover a package of agreed-upon methods, this variety should help to stimulate your imagination as you create an approach that will work for you in your particular context. For example, one answer to this question intrigued me: "I urge pastors to write at least one sermon a month in a Starbucks. Listen to the conversations around you. You will hear the questions and language of our culture."

The answers to this question were incomplete. One pastor just wrote, "They will be." Another said, "I need help here." Among the more complete answers are the following:

This is on the table. One worship coordinator, the pastors, music leader, worship assistants and the A/V Team representative. I have worked with one or two other people at times. This depends on who may be helping to plan worship. There is no formal way these people are chosen.

It includes the two pastors, the program director, and the praise band leader. At times others show up who have been invited or who are going to be involved in some way.

The group will be no larger than six. They will be chosen based upon their commitment to the vision of Salem.

Are members of the group active in the technical work of visualization during the preaching?
There were some very brief answers to this question, including "No," "Rarely," and "I hope they will be." Other answers were more complete.

At times I need people to advance the PowerPoint slides and work the computer. Other times (prior to the permanent screen being set up) I needed people to set up the screen and sound for the sanctuary.

No. At this time the technical work of visualization during the preaching event is done by crew members who are responsible for separate worship services. This means they are working from written and oral instructions and dialogue with each other between services. Often the preacher goes through the presentation with them prior to the service. While this usually happens prior to the first service, we sometimes run out of time prior to the second worship service, putting the technical crew member at a disadvantage.

So far we have trained seventeen people who take turns doing all the technical work during a service. They have full responsibility and full authority to experiment with hardware and software for the sake of improving our use of projection.

Visual Resources

The survey's next topic is the very practical matter of the sources for visual material. There is much good news here. Respondents typically indicated that they make some of their own video clips, get testimonies of faith from their people, and do on-the-street interviews, drama, and so forth. It is very clear that homemade videos presenting actual members of the congregation are received with great delight. Some pastors use photos of congregational events.

For someone with a computer and Internet access, the supply of images is practically endless, and many respondents use online resources. Some congregations get as many as 90 percent of the visuals they use from online resources. We will list a number of these online resources below.

Congregations have found many other resources as well. One respondent mentions magazines, comic strips, and newspapers. Movie clips are used extensively. One pastor mentioned that the *Seasons of the Spirit* curriculum material (published by the United Church of Christ) was often helpful. Another says she has a media guru who can find whatever she wants. Several congregations use DVDs. Artwork, of course, is frequently mentioned. One pastor refers specifically to the Smithsonian Art Gallery.

Do you make use of online resources? What online sources do you recommend?

The pastors who responded to my questionnaire get the bulk of their images from resources on the Internet. They recommended several Web sites for searching for visual images. I have perused these sites and others to determine their usefulness as image sources for preaching. In the following list of Web sites, I begin with those that seemed best to me and offer a short description of each. Although this is not a scientifically exhaustive listing, it will provide you with access to all the images you need for a lifetime of thinking in picture.

Most Web sites have a "permissions" category so that you can determine whether or not the picture you wish to use is in the public domain or permission is needed for use.

The Flaming Fire Illustrated Bible (lastditcheffort.org/~adam/FFIB /library.php): This Web site, a project that aims to offer illustrations of every Bible verse (King James Version), is a very helpful resource with easily accessible images. An easy-to-use reference chart enables you to call up any images they might have on individual passages of scripture. The images are of many types: photos, classic artwork, drawings, and so forth. They do not yet have images for every single text of the Bible, but the ability to search for images for a particular passage of scripture makes this site well suited for discovering images for preaching.

The Text This Week (textweek.com): This site provides a wealth of information for the preparation of sermons throughout the church year. It offers a variety of tools for your study of the texts appointed by the Revised Common Lectionary. There is an Art Index through which you can search for appropriate images by biblical text, theme, or date in the lectionary. A host of classic artwork is readily available to you. At times the site presents you with a variety of images on a single verse of scripture. It also provides the name of the image, the artist's name, and the date the image was created. This information helps you credit the source on the screen or in the bulletin.

Olga's Gallery (abcgallery.com): This Web site defines itself as "one of the most comprehensive online collections," featuring artists "from all around the world." The site claims to offer more than eight thousand works of art, along with information about the artists and works. You can focus your search by clicking on categories such as Ancient Greek and Roman Myths Index, Christian Saints Index, New Testament Notes, and World Literature in Painting Notes. This Web site can help you discover the great works of art from history's best artists.

Lumicon (lumicon.org): This highly creative site offers digital resources for preaching related to the Revised Common Lectionary text for the week. It recommends movie clips for most Sundays, and they can be downloaded for your use. The site is fee based.

Leonard Sweet (preachingplus.com): This Web site provides a variety of helpful tools for weekly sermon preparation. There is a link to PreachingPlus, Leonard Sweet's Web site for preaching resources, including sermon starters, children's sermons, sermon illustrations, an image bank, PowerPoint presentations, and dramas. There is an annual fee of $49.95 for access to PreachingPlus.

Google (google.com): You can specify that the popular Google search engine look only for images. To do this, you click on the hyperlink labeled "Images" and enter a word or phrase describing the kind of image you are looking for. Almost immediately, Google provides a list of links to images from throughout the World Wide Web. Several pastors have told me that this is the only Web site they ever use.

It is important to remember, however, that the quality of images and the legality of their posting varies according to the site to which you link.

AltaVista Image Search (altavista.com/image/default): Like Google, AltaVista is a search engine, and it advertises itself as offering "the largest image search on the Web." You specify the kinds of files you want to search for (all images or just photos or graphics) and type in words describing the image content you are searching for. In an instant, a list of images is available, each with a "more info" link to click to obtain the title of the image, the artist, and so forth. The images from this Web site can be downloaded in several sizes, and you can also search for video files.

FreeFoto.com (freefoto.com): This site offers more than sixty thousand photo images, free to private noncommercial users. The home page lists a number of categories; click on "Church," and you get a page promising "a selection of church images covering everything from Christmas to Easter." A site search engine makes finding the images easy. The number of religious images available on this site is limited, but what it does have may be helpful.

Hollywood Jesus (hollywoodjesus.com): This Web site's slogan is "Pop Culture from a Spiritual Point of View." As its title suggests, it focuses on movies, which it promises to examine from a Christian perspective. To try this site, I asked for more information about *Lord of the Rings: The Return of the King*. I was presented with a variety of options: reviews, trailers, photos, information about the film, cast, and crew, "spiritual connections," and a discussion forum. The photos offered from the film would work very well as accompaniment to a presentation of parts of this great story by J. R. R. Tolkien. Clicking on "spiritual connections" connected me to offerings called "spiritual quotes" and "Biblical connection." There is much, much more. This site will be of great assistance to those who want to use movies in verbal or visual ways in a sermon.

The Internet Movie Database (imdb.com): This secular site can provide all you need to know about a movie you might be considering.

The site posts movie reviews, information on the actors, background on the director, and so forth. However, it will not in and of itself help you discover a film that might work with a given text of scripture.

Hollywood.org (hollywood.org): This site gives you up-to-date information on movies playing now and yesterday. Like the Internet Movie Database, it is a secular site, so you will have to supply most of the theological connections. Reviews of movies are posted, along with easily accessible data on each movie. There is information about videos and DVDs, but no means of viewing the movies are available.

ScreenVue (screenvue.com): This site, hosted by Christian Video Licensing International, calls itself "Your Partner for Movies and Ministry." It offers sermon illustration ideas and two hundred video clips a year that are "sermon ready," so to speak. There is a fee of $135 for this service. A free fourteen-day trial period is available so that you can further check out this service.

Images of the World (imagesoftheworld.org): As its name indicates, this site catalogs "images of the world." You can easily access photos illustrating all parts of the world. The images on this site, however, are not related to Scripture.

Webshots (webshots.com): This site is a photo-sharing network and is not religious in nature. You can post photos to share, look at photos others have posted, and download images. Webshots offers many categories under which you might call up photos to browse. The photo search function is excellent, allowing you to search by artist or title. For a free membership, you may download a few free photos each day; to download more, you must pay a fee.

"Bible Study Tools," Crosswalk.com (bible.crosswalk.com): This Web site, commonly known as the "online Bible," contains no images. It does, however, provide access to the Bible in many different versions and languages. It has passage search and keyword search functions. You can print or download printer-friendly versions of results for your bulletin or for projection. This site would be very helpful if you wished to display important differences of meaning in a biblical text as revealed in varying translations.

Pitts Theology Libary Digital Image Archive (www.pitts.emory.edu /dia/searchform.cfm): This Web site provides many images from the Reformation era. Searches are by call number, topic, or scriptural reference. Details are given for the art source, description, and a scriptural reference, if appropriate. Permission is granted to use these images with credit to the Pitts Theology Library.

Reverend Fun (rev-fun.gospelcom.net/): This Web site is a cartoon resource for Christian ministry—the search engine is easy to use, and downloading of cartoons is free. The offerings are limited but what is there could be very useful in children's sermons or in the standard sermon where a bit of humor might be called for.

Of course, many more online resources exist—too many to list here. Also, Web sites are constantly in flux; some of these sites may have been terminated, and others will certainly have been created. At any rate, there will always be Web sites providing us with more possibilities of visualization than we can ever employ. One final Web site worthy of mention is DigitalChurches.com (digitalchurches. com). On this site, Pastor Robert Driver-Bishop gives basic instructions in how to begin a digital ministry.

How do you catalog visual material for possible use?

The answers to this question were surprising. Not many pastors have done work in this area. Some just left the question blank. Others said, "I need help here." One indicated that he does save images he has used in the past on computer disks. Many rely on their own memory. Another said, "I'm not sure." Others admit that they approach the matter in a random fashion.

It is important to remember that nearly all of these practitioners use online resources, and the images on the Web sites are already cataloged. With a site search engine, one enters a topic, and the Web site calls up appropriate images. I was astonished at how easy it is to do this. Still, cataloging is important. I would urge you from your beginning in this field to find ways to systematically catalog what you see that is useful. Take notes on movies you attend, and file them under an appropriate and corresponding text of the Bible or by topic or whatever will help you retrieve this material for future use. Browse the Web sites, keeping some kind of journal of what can be found there. Any course of cataloging you devise for future retrieval is fine. Just do it. In addition, a series of liturgical images relating to the church year are included on the CD-ROM accompanying this book. These images are included to help give you a starting place for thinking in picture.

What copyright issues are involved?

Here again, an assortment of answers greets us. Many respondents just say outright that they have not paid much attention as yet to this matter. One called it a "good question." One noted that the *Seasons of the Spirit* resource grants permission to use its visuals during a given time period. One congregation has hired a Contemporary Worship Consultant, who they hope will be able to deal with the copyright issue. Another respondent passes along the reminder that much older art (pre-twentieth-century) is in the public domain, although when the images are captured by professional photographers, there are copyright issues involved. Some pastors frankly ask for guidance in this area. "We've played it safe," wrote one. That's good advice.

A few have dealt seriously with this issue. "We need to be careful about copyright issues," wrote one pastor. "There is a movie license that can be purchased for about $200 (contingent on congregation size)." This pastor suggests obtaining further information from the Motion Picture Licensing Corporation (mplc.com), whose Web site answers questions related to licensing. The pastor recommends another safe course as well: "There are some sermon sites that have visuals to use without copyright concerns as long as you have a subscription to their site." (Lumicon, from the previous list, is such a site.) The pastor concludes, "With other visuals, you may need to document and footnote the information. Sometimes you need to write and ask permission. Unfortunately, there are some visuals that cannot be used."

In the appendix of his D. Min in Preaching thesis, Timothy Stidham lists the following information:

Christian Video Licensing International, 888-771-2854
www.mplc.com/index2.htm. This website is related to
www.mpls.com. [See above.]

Christian Copyright Licensing International, 1-800-234-2446, www.ccli.com [Song lyric/service taping licensing.]

Paramount Pictures Studios. www.paramount.com/studio Fax requests to: Larry McCallister, 323-862-1011.[1]

Stidham's bottom-line advice is "If in doubt, don't show it."

Congregational Response

How has your congregation responded to your use of visualization in preaching?
We will listen again to a variety of voices.

The majority of our congregation has seen our use of visualization as a blessing. Those without previous church experience respond the most favorably. We have heard a few negative remarks, such as, "It is sometimes overdone," "I don't like music videos," and "I don't like the fact that we have to darken our church."

Very favorably. They have actually purchased more equipment (electronic screen, DVD/VCR, etc.) to make the use of visual preaching easier. I receive favorable feedback from senior members to Sunday school kids. I sense that this is less of an "age" thing and more of a "learning style" thing. Some people just seem to think visually.

Majority positive. It helps them visualize the message. It draws them in and engages them. It is entertaining and memorable. There is a minority who find it distracting and too much like a business presentation. In my earlier stages this year, I did a lot with words on screen. I'm moving more toward images with fewer words.
    That, I think, is excellent advice.

They have enjoyed the use of visualization in my preaching. People will comment on the image or video clip on the way out. I also watch the response as I preach to see how it has been received. They love it mostly. . . . The people who are offended by it must keep their mouths shut, because I haven't heard anything negative. But then again—I haven't really pushed the envelope.

Our responses have been very positive. I made some unwise early choices. We need always remember that children are present.

Very well—although we have one service where we don't use the screen, which is probably why I don't use visuals more often. It's hard to prepare a sermon that is meant to include visuals and then preach that sermon without them.

Very positive. I think the variety/diversity of our use has contributed to the overwhelming positive feedback. One person expressed concern at the outset that the images would be overdone.

Very positively. The most positive response came from the people you might expect to object the most, retired people. . . . They said things like: "That was the first time in years I could read the words," "I liked seeing pictures of my old shut-in friends." As pastors we noticed that more kids were attending worship and doing so more willingly. People really are moved when we use projection to show photos of people here. . . . I think it's wonderful and essential to engage emotions and not only intellect in faith, worship, and life.

Have you intentionally sought feedback on this matter? How did you do it?

In preparing his D. Min in Preaching thesis on the matter of visualization in preaching, Pastor Tim Stidham did an elaborate survey of the congregation, using a detailed instrument of evaluation. As this is the most thorough response I have received on this matter, I will quote from Pastor Stidham at some length:

> We asked people in two identical surveys to classify their own level of spiritual growth, time with our congregation, and their previous church experience. Next, we gave a list of fourteen potential attributes of preaching and asked people to check all that applied. Next, we asked people what ways my preaching helped them draw closer to God, if any, and give space for their written responses. Next we asked how the use of multimedia has impacted preaching and worship at New Hope [Community Church of the Nazarene], listing ten descriptive terms. We also listed eight different forms of multimedia and asked people to select the one they found most compelling. Finally,

we asked for any ways I could improve my preaching, indicating that I am always looking to improve.[2]

Concerning the relationship between his preaching and the use of multimedia, Pastor Stidham reports that the majority of responses were positive. More than 60 percent felt that the messages and/or the media clips were relevant. Many indicated growth in their faith life as a result of his preaching. The responses people made to Pastor Stidham about the sermons were far more specific than any he had received in the past. People anticipated what was coming next and came to church with a feeling of anticipation. The most popular visual material was his use of movie clips, which 70 percent of his congregation favored highly, followed by music videos (favored by 65 percent), on-screen scripture (around 60 percent), and prerecorded contemporary music (around 50 percent).[3] Video interviews were also highly appreciated. As we have said before, congregants seemed to enjoy very much seeing pictures of themselves on screen.

Given the positive response to movie clips in sermons, Pastor Stidham makes a point of recommending their use to others. People experienced the movie clips and other visual images as tying his sermons to everyday life and helping to make scripture and a relationship with God seem more viable. People were able to describe in some detail the impact of the multimedia experience on their life of faith. Perhaps most important, the scripture never took a backseat to the media experience. Scripture remained for people the main source of inspiration, with the media facilitating the message of scripture. Congregational members became more interested in Bible study as a response to his preaching. According to Pastor Stidham, the use of movie clips, for example, hadn't made respondents more enamored of culture, but rather more enamored with the Bible. This is a very important point. Any use of multimedia visualization in preaching should have the goal of facilitating the biblical message. Images complement the words of scripture. Images and words used together seem to make a greater impact on people's lives than images or words alone.

In response to my survey, one pastor wrote that he has asked various people about their response and what kinds of things they had heard from others. He said every response he heard was positive about the use of visuals.

Another pastor indicated that she had not intentionally sought feedback. She said that if she sought feedback, she would use anonymous feedback forms. Another had been engaged in the visualization process for only eight months and said the time for formal evaluation had not yet come.

How have you dealt with opponents of visualization?

I haven't run into any in my congregation (yet). . . . The disciples in the pews that I have encountered think it helps them understand the sermon better and have indicated that it enhances their worship experience. I get frustrated with the opponents (other pastors, seminary professors), but I am not deterred. . . . What about the people who are searching and have yet to find what they are looking for? What if the communication of the Good News hasn't connected with them in a way that makes sense yet? If use of visuals can be used as a tool to enable somebody to experience the Gospel of Jesus Christ for the first time or in a new way . . . then it is absolutely worth persevering and moving ahead.

I have responded by softening and reducing the amount of images. They want to hear me better, and some can't multitask.

We have had no opponents. This may sound unrealistic, but people have not complained about visualization in the sermons. I believe this is because we do not try and fit visualization into worship, but we let the visualization grow out of the worship and the sermon. No one has ever asked me why I used that visual. It has to be integrated, and obvious connections must be apparent.

The biggest obstacle was what the screen/projector would look like in the sanctuary. We opted for a screen that can be hidden in a "soffit" so as not to disturb the beauty of the sanctuary. . . . The projector, unfortunately, will be a permanent mount, and it will hang from the ceiling.

There have been a few objectors. We need to communicate to the congregation on many levels the rationale for what we are doing.

In one instance I responded to a concern by reassuring the individual that we have this technology as a creative way to accomplish God's purpose and communicate the Gospel. It is simply one means to this greater end and not an end in itself. We have committed to use this technology as a way to serve the Word. I believe our commitment to connect the use of image with scripture and to do this with variety, quality, and creativity has nurtured enthusiasm for and minimized opposition to the use of this technology in worship and preaching.

There were very few and predictable. We can safely ignore them here. This has been the case since a big rumble six years ago when we started making changes. Then the issue was "contemporary music." The congregation then had to get clear about who made decisions, why and how they got made, and what was acceptable/unacceptable behavior. Although very hard, the fight cleared up those issues and made for a really healthy church. Some of the negative people did leave the church.

Pastor-to-Pastor Advice

What is the most important advice you would give to pastors who are considering using visualization in preaching?
Here again, the pastors responding to the questionnaire offered a grand variety of advice. Some wrote long, some wrote short.

First and foremost: Pray about it. And then do this only for the sake of God being able to use you though this.
1. *Help key leaders and the congregation understand what and why.*
2. *Get the hardware right. Get experienced design help. Don't be cheap.*
3. *Get the right software. (Song Show is really good.)*
4. *Train users well.*
5. *Knock their socks off when first using it.*
6. *It must be consistently well-done. That probably means starting out simply and adding as you learn. A few mistakes are okay. But it always has to flow.*
7. *It must be sustainable. You need enough trained people so that no one or few are asked to do more than their busy lives can handle. So far, five months into projection, we have seventeen trained users. I think we need twenty-five.*

Don't try to be cheap on equipment.

Take your time when introducing visuals to the congregation. Don't run out and purchase $8,000 worth of equipment without having first introduced visuals to the congregation. This has resulted in failure in various congregations. In these instances I believe congregation members were seeing the dollar signs instead of the projected images, and the Gospel was clouded over as a result. Starting with an overhead or slide projector is good. . . . Borrowing or renting an LCD projector from time to time will allow your congregation members to see more possibilities. After all of this, presenting a proposal for equipment purchase might be better received.

One thing that has worked well is being able to bridge the gap between events that happen in the parish and the sermon—faith and life. We sent 20 kids to Chicago to do a service project for a week. Armed with digital pictures of our kids at work, I was able to preach about how living out of our faith we were called to serve and use stories and pictures of our congregation in action.

Another thing that has worked well is the use of movie clips in sermons. When the illustration fits, this can be especially powerful. Look how many people go to the movies. . . . Movies portray the human condition, evil, hope, love, and grace. Utilizing them in our preaching is one more way to bridge the gap from Sunday to Monday. We can now take what people are thinking and talking about in their 9–5 workaday lives and rework it in a theological worldview where everything relates to God.

It has been an incredible blessing to my preaching. It has moved me to a more incarnational place. Choose pictures carefully, use judiciously, crop or enlarge for effect, watch too much use of PowerPoint effects, start with images first sometimes, as God speaks through them, too. Remember that PowerPoint is linear, one slide after another. Postmoderns are less linear. I try to bring more circularity by returning to key images throughout and at the end. Don't let the visuals take over. I face this temptation every week. You will get better at it.

One Tech Tip: research equipment carefully.

Don't use visuals because the church growth people tell you it is what is needed to reach certain people. Don't make visuals fit into what you are doing. Use visuals because they truly enhance what you are preaching. Use a visual because it helps explain or enhance what you are saying. Use a video clip because it is a great example or story for this sermon. I believe one of the reasons the people who like traditional worship value the visual technology is because I use it when it truly enhances the sermon and I don't use it just to use it. Let the creative Spirit of God work in and through you to touch people's souls in a variety of ways through your sermons.

As of now, since I'm at the beginning, the best advice is to communicate, communicate, communicate the vision.

I would like to say don't make a big deal of it. If it naturally enhances the proclamation of the Gospel, it will work and people will be open to it. If you force it—which I've seen way too much of—it can become corny and do a disservice to the Gospel.

The leadership of your church must understand what you are doing and support you. In our situation we should have invested more in our sound system. The use of visualization distinguishes us in our community and works well for outreach purposes.

Get at least one person to work with you. My original goal was to have a multimedia team formed from members of the original task force, but my first year as a pastor has been so hectic that I haven't had time to focus on multimedia the way I wanted to.

Look to the scripture/text as a foundation for images. Let the image be the means to the greater end of communicating the gospel. Continually look for gifts among people in the congregation as a resource for the development of a support team. Provide detailed script/instructions for the members of the team who will be operating the equipment. Look to events in the daily life of individuals and congregation as a source for images related to the text and the message . . . death, birth, marriage etc. Seek a balance between images from the Internet and those taken of members/events in your own community of faith.

Wisdom from the Classroom

I have had the privilege of teaching a course that dealt in part with thinking in picture. The students who ventured into that course were eager to try out this new possibility for preaching, and they entered into the spirit of the course with great energy and creativity. Each student preached two sermons with visualization. The first sermon they did on their own. A few of the sermons were low-tech. Most used some kind of projected images. One had a movie clip, others let images flow as companions to their spoken words, some focused on two or three projected images, and one used several paintings that he himself had painted. For the second sermon, they worked in groups of three to four. These sermons were marked with the same type of variety of images. I went home from class one day and told my wife how wonderful the sermons had been in class that day. "I wish you could have *seen* them," I said. The words just spilled out of my mouth unconsciously. I had never before in my life talked about *seeing* a sermon. I realized that I was, indeed, learning how to think in picture.

At the end of the term, I asked each student to write three sentences' worth of advice that they would give to a parish pastor who asked them about how to use visuals in preaching. Some of their responses to this query plus other responses they made during the term of the course are as follows:

Don't be afraid and don't try to do too much the first time.

Begin sermon preparation as you normally would—figure out what it is you're trying to communicate, and then look at the most effective way to communicate that.

Make sure you are comfortable with the visual (because if you're not, the congregation won't be either).

Maintain a clear connection between the image and what is being said.

When it comes to using visuals in preaching, it is better to do something simple and do it well, rather than to do something potentially flashy or technologically leading-edge and carry it off poorly.

Visual arts do not make a good sermon. Visual arts make a good sermon better.

Keep it simple; less is generally more.

Practice, practice, practice to avoid any technical glitches; and be sure to view the visuals from the point of view of the congregation to make sure they are visible.

Any art that is to function as community art need not be defined in words, but it does need to restrict itself to visual elements that are comprehensible to the community.

Consider putting your visualized sermons on your church's Web site.

Think of pictures as mini-incarnations.

Music can also be used with the pictures. Music and pictures probably massage the right brain; words massage the left brain. In practice these two do not come into conflict, making it hard to follow so much stimuli. The engagement of the whole brain may actually give the listener/viewer greater focus and concentration.

The selection of images needs to be very carefully done, taking into account racial, ethnic, gender, and age balance and sensitivity.

It may be good at times when using multiple images to let the screen go blank between images to avoid confusion.

When your sermon is imaged on the screen, you have your notes for preaching right there before you. You don't need any notes of your own.

Avoid a steady diet of pictures that need to be explained. Such usage is really a left-brain exposition of ideas.

Keep your usage of media personal/communal vs. impersonal mass media.

Try it, you'll like it.

One matter that we discussed much in class was the evocative power of images. Images evoke a variety of connotations in people's minds. This relates to my earlier discussion of the *diffuseness* of images. Images can have no boundaries, meaning a variety of things to a variety of people. Of course, this can be true of our words of preaching as well. Any pastor who has researched the sermons actually "heard" in her congregation in contrast to what she intended to say knows that just about everyone hears a different sermon. When visualization is used, people *see* different sermons as well. Given that much about our preaching is out of our control, how do we as pastors deal with that? We must remind ourselves of the role of the Holy Spirit in preaching. Is it not the Spirit's task to apply the word *seen* and *heard* to individual lives and hearts? Martin Luther said it well when he put words into the Spirit's mouth to advise us about preaching: "You preach, let me manage."

Part of the elusiveness of preaching with images is that images often take time to settle in the human mind. Many pastors who preach visualized sermons have experienced parishioners commenting to them that it wasn't until Wednesday or Thursday or whatever day after the sermon was seen and heard that the images began to take hold in their consciousness. Only after many days of reflection did the image hit home. Therefore, as pastors, we cannot expect that when parishioners shake our hand at the door of the church, they will always tell us what the images in the sermon meant to them. We are again reminded that much of what happens in visualized sermons is simply beyond our control. We cannot avoid this "image delay." We must simply acknowledge that, indeed, so very much in our preaching is beyond our control. "You preach, let me manage."

5

Sermon Structures

To USE VISUAL IMAGES in preaching, we must determine the kinds of sermons into which these images can be incorporated. Do we need to change our entire way of thinking about preaching, or can we simply integrate visual images into our present form of sermon preparation? After some years of teaching homiletics, I have concluded that there are three basic types of sermons, which I defined in the introduction to this book as thinking in idea, thinking in story, and thinking in image. We can use visual images in each of these sermon types. Images work differently in each sermonic form, but each form can be enhanced through visualization.

In general, visuals can work together with the spoken word to accomplish one of at least three tasks. If we think of scripture as the ground of the sermon, visualization can be used to *illustrate* the text, *apply* the text to the lives of the hearers, or be *juxtaposed* to the text so the congregation can see and hear the text from a different angle.

This variety of uses for visuals accompanying a sermon is important because the listeners come to the homiletic encounter with different ways of learning. This diversity within the congregation also provides an argument for using a variety of sermon forms: idea, story, and image. Another reason for variety in sermons comes from the education theory of multiple intelligences. Dr. Howard Gardner, professor of education at Harvard University, proposes eight different intelligences, which people possess to different degrees. He hypothesizes that people have various levels of each intelligence, that is, different degrees of ability to learn through different means. Individuals may be word smart, number/reasoning smart, picture smart, body smart, music smart, people smart, self smart, and nature smart. As preachers think about communicating to any congregation, they must remember that this grand variety of "smart" people is occupying the pews. The variety among people demands of the preacher a variety of sermonic approaches.

Thinking in Idea

As I pointed out in part I, the Western world of philosophical or intellectual thought has largely preferenced poetry over painting and words over ideas. It should not be surprising, therefore, that the basic approach to preaching over the past several hundred years has been geared to ideas. (Plato would be proud of us.) What is sometimes facetiously referred to as "three points and a poem" has been our basic sermon structure for centuries. This sermon structure received its most serious challenge in the latter part of the twentieth century with the rise of what is often referred to as "the New Homiletics." This unorganized polymorphic movement has offered several alternatives to thinking in idea as the assumed form of a sermon. One of those alternatives, of course, is thinking in story. Still, the basic explanatory structure of preaching probably continues to dominate the Sunday-morning sermon time in our land.

Thinking in idea as a sermon structure simply refers to the core structure of the sermon being the careful arrangement of ideas. I was taught this approach to preaching in the 1950s. The preacher proceeds either to find the one basic "big idea" in the text and develop three subpoints to explicate the central idea or to find three ideas in the text that will form the three points of the sermon.

The faith engendered by preaching that majors in ideas will be faith defined by cognition. Once the hearer understands the ideas in the text, that hearer can believe in the truth of the propositions propounded. I must say that the Lutheran Church in which I was raised and nourished majored in faith as assent to truth. Ideas reigned. As a young teacher/preacher, I knew only one thing to do, whether I was teaching or preaching. My single goal was to put ideas into people's heads. No one had ever suggested to me that there might be other possibilities for teaching and preaching.

Illustrations do have a role in preaching as thinking in idea. Following the lead of John Dominic Crossan, I have referred to such imagery as *metaphors of illustration*.[1] A metaphor of illustration seeks to illustrate the point at hand and then should recede from thought. Its purpose is to help hearers grasp the point, so once the point is understood, the metaphor is dispensable. The focus should be on the idea, not the illustration, the temporary aid to understanding. When preaching thinks in idea, this is the usual purpose of visual images—that is, for a temporary impact serving the larger goal of aiding the hearer in understanding the point being made. There is nothing wrong with this usage of visual images.

On one occasion, I heard an excellent sermon on the story of the prodigal son in Luke 15. From the outset of the sermon, there was a projected work of classic art portraying the father's welcome of the son. It was not explained; it was just there. We all knew that this image was grounded in the text. The point of the sermon that day was to underscore the significant fact that the welcome of the son was not just the experience of the individual whom we call "prodigal," but rather a *communal* experience. After all, the father threw a big party. When the pastor came to make his point through the closing verses of the story, he projected a second visual image, another classic work of art. It depicted the father, the son, the people bringing the calf and the "best robe" for the son to wear, and others—the corporate welcome of the son. This is a very important theological point. God does not just welcome us as individuals into the kingdom. God welcomes us into a new community! The visual images made this point strongly and memorably. I saw and will never forget the point of that sermon. The images had done their work.

I've "seen" other sermons where visual images were projected to parallel each of the major points of the sermon with a corresponding picture. One might call this a kind of double-track sermon. One track is the preacher's explanation of the text and its ideas. A second track features projected images that illustrate the point being made. Words are illustrated by images. Images accompany words. This can be a very effective way of getting one's points across. It doesn't matter that multiple images are more forgettable and dispensable than a single image projected during a sermon, because the goal is to get across the idea. Once the images have served their purpose, they are dispensable. The images were used for illustrative purposes.

The illustrative role of images is important, because it supports thinking in idea, the dominant mode of preaching in the Christian community for hundreds of years. Images illustrate points very well at times; they can help people visualize the ideas being presented. This use of visual images in preaching is significant but is by no means the only helpful use of images in the preaching context.

Thinking in Story

The use of story has experienced resurgence in preaching over the course of the last twenty years or so. What we have described as the New Homiletic has set forth a variety of forms of storytelling for preaching.[2] In my book *Telling the Story*, I set forth the possibility of story sermons. In my initial conception of storytelling and preaching, I described this form of preaching as the creation of a story, which one could lay out alongside the text. The preacher creates or discovers a story that can be told as the sermon. The conclusion of the preacher's story links that story to the text given or chosen for that Sunday. The preacher might then explicate the nature of the intertwining of the two stories or leave the two stories (textual story and sermon story) open, allowing the hearers, guided by the Holy Spirit, to reach their own conclusions.

In such an enterprise, faith is much more about recognition than cognition. The hearers recognize themselves in the juxtaposition of stories and see the implication for their own lives. In this case, the listeners' imaginative participation in the sermon is vitally important to the life and impact of the sermon.

In this form of sermon, visual images would play a different role than they would in a sermon based on thinking in ideas. Instead of having a primarily illustrative role (as metaphors of illustration), the images used with stories of almost any kind would be *metaphors of participation*. The images would function to enhance our participation in the stories told.

This use of images fits the goal of storytelling. Instead of putting *ideas* into people's heads, preaching through stories is intended to put *people* into the minds and hearts of the hearers (especially bibli-

cal people, such as Adam and Eve, Abraham and Sarah, Moses and
Miriam, Jesus and Mary). This objective is true in each of the forms
of storytelling that I will briefly describe.

Retelling the Story

As I mentioned at the beginning of this section, the preacher may
create a story that is juxtaposed with the text. Another approach is
to retell the biblical story itself. Eugene Lowry has proposed four
structures for such storytelling sermons in his book *How to Preach
a Parable.*[3] Although this book is about preaching on biblical parables, this definition can be stretched to cover any type of biblical
story. Lowry's four structures for biblical stories are as follows:

1. *Running the story.* This type of sermon is composed solely of
   the retelling of the biblical story, leading to an application as its
   conclusion.
2. *Delaying the story.* The sermon does not begin with the biblical
   story but delays its telling. First, the preacher sets a context for
   hearing the biblical story. The preacher gives the listeners some
   background information or some story from daily life that
   will prepare them to hear the biblical story and the sermon's
   application.
3. *Suspending the story.* This type of preaching begins with the
   telling of the biblical story, but the preacher suspends the telling of this story for some explanation of a word in the text,
   some contextual reference that helps to understand the story,
   or some other information before returning to the biblical
   story and the application of the sermon.
4. *Alternating the story.* In this form of preaching, two things
   occur side by side. The preacher alternates telling the biblical story with telling a contemporary story or a contemporary
   context or an idea that connects to the biblical story at this
   point. In a way, this approach uses the biblical story as a means
   to apply the story to several different life situations. The biblical story provides the shape of the sermon, and it is alternated
   with content aimed at explicating ideas illustrated by the story.
   This can be a very effective means of teaching a biblical story.

With the first three methods, visual images are likely to be used as metaphors of participation. Visual images used with alternating the story may parallel more closely the use of images as metaphors of illustration.

Stitching Stories

In *Thinking in Story*, I set forth ways of stitching stories together in order to form a sermon. From the practice of teaching homiletics, I have discovered other stitching possibilities. A form of story-stitching sermons that has worked very well in my classroom experience can be diagramed as follows:

Introduction⟶Stories⟶Human Condition⟶Proclamation of the Gospel

INTRODUCTION. The introduction functions primarily to capture the congregation's attention and to provide a rationale for why you are going to tell the stories of your sermon. Usually that rationale is based in the nature of the human condition that the sermon will seek to interpret. That condition may be guilt, hopelessness, sin, grief, or any number of the afflictions of the human condition of life on earth. The introduction presents one such reality and invites the congregation to listen to the following stories as a way of explicating both the difficult human reality and the hopeful divine possibility related to the human condition.

STORIES. The body of this type of sermon is its stories. If the biblical text is in story form, that story is the most important one to tell. In my class, the first sermon that I assign students to preach requires them to tell only biblical stories in this section of the sermon.

The work of narrative critics in our time has demonstrated to us that most Bible stories do not live in isolation from other biblical stories. Robert Alter, a Jewish critic of literature who has applied his methods to the Bible, calls this "narrative analogy."[4] Biblical writers, he contends, are constantly locking their stories together with other stories from that book of the Bible or other parts of the Bible. It is not difficult, therefore, to discover other biblical stories that complement, complete, fulfill, and add resonance to the story at hand. In books on the Synoptic Gospels, I have demonstrated links between the gospel stories assigned in the lectionary system and the stories in the remainder of a particular Gospel. Preaching as this kind of biblical storytelling is incredibly powerful.[5]

Besides linking the biblical story to other biblical stories, the preacher can also stitch it together with other narratives. Possibilities include stories from autobiography, biography, stories of individuals and communities of faith, stories from the arts, creative fiction, current events, or events in nature in order to bring the biblical story to life and focus.

A requirement that distinguishes story preaching from preaching that thinks in idea is that it ought to have only one point or one center. The stories told should not add new points to the sermon but should amplify, clarify, intensify the central thrust of the textual story. In this sense, storytelling is not economical. You can make several points in the time it takes to tell one or two stories.

Another difference occurs between the goal of ideas and the goal of stories. As I have said, the goal of ideas in preaching is to reach understanding; the goal of stories is to elicit participation.

In the part of the sermon that tells stories, the central thrust of those stories would normally focus on the action of God on behalf of the humans in the stories. The stories should bring alive the reality of God acting in, with, and under the reality of human lives. Each story should amplify the graciousness of God in relation to an aspect of the human condition. Our preaching is to be centered in "good news." *Christian* preaching is the announcement of the good news that God has intervened in human history in the birth, life, ministry, death, and resurrection of Jesus Christ. Our stories should make clear the promises of God for the various conditions of humanity. Promise is central to such preaching.

HUMAN CONDITION. The next section of the sermon should deal with the human condition in more depth. Whether or not the introduction referred to that condition, this is the time to explicate the human predicament. Our predicament is probably as varied as the populace of the human race. Some of the most common human predicaments are sin, being "sinned against" (oppression), guilt, shame, lack of identity, purposelessness, hopelessness, despair, and grief. Related to each of these conditions are gospel themes, actions, and promises of God. Normally, a sermon would treat only one of these themes. There are a number of ways to explicate these conditions. For instance, the preacher might tell stories of humans who exemplify one of these predicaments or might list ways in which one of these conditions is manifest in our lives.

The goal of describing the human condition is to help the listeners come to grips with ways in which the predicament of this sermon affects their individual lives. We invite our congregants to see themselves as sinners or as guilt-laden beings or as grief-stricken persons and so forth. We lead them toward awareness, identification, confession, or repentance—whichever reality best suits individual listeners. Specifically, we hope to lead our congregants to a level of self-awareness that helps them identify with both the predicament evident in the stories we have told and the God who has come to help us in our predicament.

One great advantage of using stories to bring about these responses in our hearers is that stories help people toward self-realization. By hearing the stories we tell, our listeners see themselves and their needs in a new light. This approach is often more helpful than trying to tell people what their predicament is. We often resist what we are told. We are more open to see ourselves for what we are when stories invite us into their world and let us draw our own conclusions.

A WORD OF PROMISE. The climax of this type of story sermon is the announcement of a promise of God addressed to the human condition. As preachers, we are now called upon to *speak for God.* Speaking for God is a common thread of Christian ministry. For example, speaking for God occurs when baptism and the Eucharist are celebrated in our midst. The presider at baptism promises us that this is the water of life in which we are reborn. The presider at Holy Communion promises us that the bread and wine are in reality the body and blood of Christ. The presider speaks, we trust the word that is spoken, and we are reborn and reimaged in Christ's form. Faith in the word of promise makes it so.

Similarly, in Martin Luther's *Small Catechism*, a section titled "The Office of the Keys" describes an "office" grounded in the story of Peter's confession of Jesus as the Christ, as told in Matthew 16:13–20. In response to Peter's confession, Jesus gives Peter the "keys of the kingdom of heaven," so that whatever Peter looses on earth is loosed in heaven and whatever he binds on earth is bound in heaven. In other words, Peter's promissory words have the power to speak a word of forgiveness to sinners, and their sins are forgiven in heaven. Forgiveness happens when an ear hears and believes a promissory word. The church grants the power of this promissory word primarily to those who lead congregations, but in an "emergency," any of the baptized can speak this word of promise to another.

This is very much the nature of preaching: speaking promissory words of God to people in need of such a promise. This concept is very different from preaching as an exchange of ideas. In this sense, the climax of story sermons is the proclamation of a promissory word of God.

The nature of that proclamation will depend on the action of God in the text of scripture that is the basis of the sermon. The specific metaphors of the text will suggest which promise of God to proclaim. A sermon preached on Mark 5:1–13, for example, might deal with the subject of possession. We as human beings are possessed by many "demons." The main stories of the sermon will demonstrate how God relates to possession. In the text, Jesus says to the man possessed by an unclean spirit, "Come out of the man, you unclean spirit!" God in Jesus Christ spoke a promissory word, and the demons fled. Our sermon on this text will tell other stories from the Bible or from daily life where God has likewise cast out unclean spirits. The human condition section of the sermon tries to lead the listener to see how his or her own life is "possessed." The climax of the sermon will be promissory words, shaped normally in first or second person, present tense language, speaking for God. Based on this text from Mark, the promissory words might be "I, Jesus Christ, have power over unclean spirits. I have power over every form of evil possession. I therefore say to the powers that enslave, 'Spirits, come out. Come out of each and every one of you. This is my command.' Go forth from this place today and live a life of freedom."

With other scriptural texts, the closing words we speak for God will be very different. Some texts will lead us to the promissory word "Your sins are forgiven." Other texts will lead to the promissory word "I am the resurrection and the life. Those who believe in me, even though they die, will live, and everyone who lives and believes in me will never die" (John 11:25-26). The Bible is filled with the promises of God. Preaching can have no higher calling than announcing these promises to all so that they may hear and believe. As Luther once said, "You preach, let me manage."

Visual Images with Story-Centered Sermons

With story-centered sermons, we have a grand variety of possibilities for the use of visual images. Probably the most obvious visual aid is to use a movie clip. According to preachers who use visual images, movie clips are one of the most highly accepted of all visual images. In story sermons, the movie clip can tell one of the stories.

Let me give just one example. In Matthew 21:28–32, Jesus confronts the chief priests and elders with a question. They have asked him about the source of his authority (Matthew 21:23–27), and Jesus replies by asking them about two sons. One son told his father he would not go to work in the father's vineyard. Afterward, he repented and did go to work. The second son spoke a good game; he said he would work in the vineyard. But he never reported for duty. "Now," says Jesus, "which of these sons do you think did the will of the father?" They answer, "The first." And Jesus says, "Truly, I say to you, the tax collectors and the harlots go into the kingdom of God before you." Jesus notes that the response of the tax collectors and harlots, the sinners, who repented in his presence, is a far greater response to his ministry than that of the chief priests and elders who did not repent.

A wonderful clip from the movie *The Fighting Temptations* could be used with this text. In this movie, Cuba Gooding Jr. is a rather no-account advertising executive living in the big city. He is informed of a death in his family, so he returns to his small hometown in Georgia. To his great surprise, he receives $150,000 from the deceased on the condition that he take the local church choir to a state contest. He hears the choir sing at the funeral and is impressed. He decides to take on the challenge. To his chagrin, he then learns that the choir he heard was not the choir he is to direct. The choir he is to direct has very few members and sings pitifully. One day in the barbershop, he hears the barbers singing and invites them to the choir. He also invites a woman of questionable reputation in town, thereby risking the wrath of some of the choir members. This woman, played by Beyonce Knowles, adds a tremendous voice to the choir. Gooding takes his vastly improved choir to sing at a nearby jail because he needs the approval of an official there to help him get into the state singing contest (he was late with his application). The inmates like what they hear, and so does the official, although the official comments that he has better singers in his prisons. "You do," Gooding says, eyes brightening. In the next scene, three convicts, chained together and wearing orange prison suits, have joined the rehearsal. A prison guard stands by with a shotgun.

In the climax of the movie—and this is the scene I would use for this sermon—Gooding's choir sings at the contest. They don't have robes to match the other choirs, so they sing in their very plain clothes, even prison clothes. When I saw the movie and watched that choir sing, the text from Matthew 21 came immediately to my mind. Here is a wonderful choir filled with repentant sinners. No tax collectors there, but there are convicts. No certain prostitute, but one woman with a questionable reputation. What a wonderful picture of the kingdom of heaven! The song they sing is "I Am Not Worthy." It's a gospel song, so these words are repeated over and over again: "I am not worthy." "Truly, I say to you," Jesus said, "the tax collectors and harlots go into the kingdom of God before you."

Besides scenes from commercial movies, a great amount of church-produced art will work especially well with biblical stories. The whole world of classical art is available to use in accompaniment with given texts. You can use just one picture or a variety of pictures to accompany the word of preaching. Also, many movies produced on religious themes can be easily used as visual stories for your sermon. A whole variety of films today enact biblical stories. They can be very useful as well. Films like the ones in the Veggie Tales series would work very well for a children's sermon. Children and the whole congregation can be amused and informed by these clever "tales." I recommend using the children's sermon to tell one of the stories of your sermon.

Visuals that tell a story and visuals that accompany a story can give our storytelling deeper appeal to the imagination. Words and images used together can touch many aspects of the listener. In the best of worlds, this combination of words and images can make a powerful holistic impact on our viewers/hearers.

Thinking in Image

The third type of preaching is what I call thinking in image. This book is centered on the use of *visual* images in preaching, what we've called "thinking in picture." Through the ages, however, *verbal* images have been most commonly associated with preaching. One dictionary definition of *image* is "a figure of speech especially a metaphor or simile." A simile compares one thing to another: God is *like* a mighty fortress. A metaphor uses one thing to describe another: God *is* a mighty fortress. A story, in turn, is an extended metaphor. We tell a story in which we reveal that God is, indeed, a mighty fortress.

A sermon moves into the category of "thinking in image" when the image itself becomes the organizing center of the sermon. The preacher, that is, uses the image as the heart and soul of the sermon. The images used to construct the sermon may be verbal and/or visual.

According to Robert Farrar Capon, we too often read scripture in an overly literal manner. A literal reading of scripture concerns itself primarily with ideas, but Capon says the Holy Spirit weaves together *images*, not *ideas,* in shaping the Bible: "All that wildly various wet-wash is hung on a paradoxical clothesline of imagery, not on a string of uniform propositional truths. The Bible is held together by *icons*, by word pictures like Light, Word, Water, Marriage, the Garden, the Tree, the Blood of Abel. . . . It is these icons, these sacraments of the real presence of the Word himself, that make [the Bible] whole."[6] Capon is particularly interested in the parables of the Bible as "imaginal stories" that "catch a glimpse of the outrageous paradoxical God they represent. Read them that way, and you'll find a richness of salvation by grace that you haven't seen before."[7] But, he laments, "The liberalism that surrounds us has so steeped our minds in the logic of propositional statements that we've lost our ability to hear anything addressed to the logic of the imagination. Consequently, we miss the point of almost everything Jesus has to say—because it's the logic of images that makes his parables stick."[8]

Capon writes that when we think in images, we read the Bible in a way that leaves us free to disagree with each other about the reality to which the image points. As earlier chapters observed, visual images can be diffuse. They speak in different ways to different people. According to Capon, the same is true of verbal images. Verbal images speak different things to different individuals. The advantage of plastic images is that those who perceive the images can relate them to their own condition of life. The disadvantage of images—verbal and visual—is that they can communicate multiple and contradictory realities to the perceiver. Images, therefore, need the kind of boundaries that come from a more literal approach to reality. Images need words for definition. Words need images for depth and mystery.

Patricia Wilson-Kastner writes that when we express our awareness in images, pictures, and stories, we take intuition into account and give more centrality to human emotions. Considering imagery to include "the whole physical and sensory dimension of the world portrayed in a sermon," including its choice of words, Wilson-Kastner assigns significant roles to both imagery and narrative: "Narrative is a primary focus for the more temporally conscious mind, imagery a focus for the spatially and visually directed."[9]

In his helpful discussion of using images in preaching, David Schlafer observes a constant interplay of image, story, and idea in the biblical material. He does not find this surprising: "The literary genres of poetry, narrative and expository argument are not arbitrary categories. These genres are natural expressions of the different . . . ways in which human beings 'make sense' of their experience. . . . Poetry is centered in image language. Narratives are centered in story language. Expository prose and persuasive oratory are centered in idea, or argument language."[10] Given these different expressions of biblical material, Schlafer goes on to challenge preachers to create sermons that "resonate with" each type of expression: "This involves more than being able to recognize the dynamics of image, story, and idea when one hears and sees them . . . . Rather, it involves being able to shape whole sermons in accordance with the distinctive timbres and interplaying tonalities of each distinctive mode of experience and language."[11]

In the case of preaching that uses verbal images, Schlafer says the goal of such preaching is to share impressions and evoke sensory images. The preacher, so to speak, stands behind the hearer so that the hearer can focus on the image itself. The hope is that the listener will make fresh sensory associations and grasp the illuminating connections between what may appear to be unrelated images. The preacher's goal is to capture the hearer's attention and stimulate the impressionistic aspect of the human imagination.

Structuring an Image Sermon

Clearly, there are numerous ways to structure a sermon built around verbal and visual images. The central metaphor for the whole sermon would be a visual image or a verbal image (from the Bible, the world of the arts, or a story of daily life). That image is so vital for the sermon that it becomes its central focus. Normally, a sermon centered in image ought to confine itself to a single image and strive to reach a singular purpose—no three points and a poem here, but a singular image, a singular goal. The sermon structure for image-based sermons might have four parts:

1. The source of the image
2. A move to scripture
3. A relevant aspect of the human condition
4. Proclamation of God's promise

THE IMAGE. In this structure, the sermon begins with the preacher explaining the source of the image, be it visual or verbal. This first section of the sermon brings the image, visual or verbal, to life for the hearers. The image may come from scripture. "The LORD is my shepherd" is an example of a strong biblical image. To use this image, the preacher begins by unfolding this image from its context in Psalm 23.

Other images come from the world of the arts. One image I have used quite often is from Andrew Lloyd Webber's *The Phantom of the Opera.* The Phantom has a deep love for a woman named Christine, who sings with the opera company. He gives her singing lessons. Eventually he invites her to join him in making "the music of the night." He invites her to join him because he loves her deeply. He expresses his love with the phrase "you alone can make my song take flight." That phrase is a verbal image.

So far, in considering visual images in preaching, we have assumed that visuals are something we add to the words of the sermon. At times, however, we discover a visual image that seems significant enough to be the main focus of the sermon. When that is the case, we may wish to begin with that visual piece, give its background, help our viewers place it in their minds. I would suggest, for example, that Michelangelo's classic sculpture the *Pietà* might well serve as the central focus of one's sermon. The *Pietà* presents Mary holding the limp body of her Son, the crucified Jesus, in her arms. Her face is strained with grief.

Connection to Scripture. From this introduction, the sermon moves to scripture. If the image already comes from scripture, then this task has been performed. That would be the case in using the image of a shepherd from the Twenty-third Psalm.

In contrast, the image from *The Phantom of the Opera* needs to be connected to scripture. In using this image, I have connected it to the story of the man with the withered hand in Mark 3:1–6. I imagine the man with the withered hand sulking around the temple with his hand hidden up his sleeve. He "masks" his wound from sight as the Phantom masks his face to hide his infirmity. Therein lies the link to scripture. The sermon will reveal more of this link to scripture when it invites us to imagine the man's response to Jesus' healing touch.

It is certainly not difficult to connect Michelangelo's *Pietà* (see page 90) to scripture. As with so many of the great works of art, it is in and of itself an exposition of scripture. We can help to explain how the work of art captures aspects of the biblical story. The *Pietà* would prompt us to help people experience the imaginative exposition of the biblical story, which moves us from Mary's cradling of the boy in swaddling clothes to the cradling of an expired Savior. If a second image were to be used with the *Pietà*, it might well be any of the classic works of art that depict Mary caressing the infant Jesus.

The Human Condition. We next show an aspect of the human condition that is demonstrated for us through the image. With "The Lord is my shepherd," influenced by a parable of Jesus, we might focus on the condition of lost sheep. In what ways are we like sheep that have lost their way in life?

The human condition that comes to mind with the image of masks from the *Phantom* is the myriad ways we choose to "mask" ourselves. So often, we mask our wounds and scars to hide them from others. We pretend our way through life. We hide our real nature even from those closest to us. Like the Phantom, we long for someone to come along who can transform our life, who can "make our song take flight." The Phantom's deepest longing was to be loved for himself. We all eagerly await the one who would love us just as we are—one, that is, who can "make our song take flight."

The visual image of Madonna and the Crucified One can be used to remind people that the religious leaders of his world would one day kill this babe of Bethlehem. One of the ways the Bible helps us understand the crucifixion is to interpret it as the reality that Jesus Christ died for our sins. The visual image might, therefore, lead us to self-examination of our own sinful ways in life. It was our sin that thrust this Jesus into Mary's arms.

PROCLAIMING THE PROMISE. Finally, we need to move from the image to the proclamation of the promise of God. In each case, the language of the promise of God is shaped by the image and by the description of the associated human condition. With the image of the Good Shepherd from the twenty-third Psalm, the move to promissory proclamation is rather obvious. As preachers, we come to the moment of proclamation, saying, "God's word for you today through this magnificent psalm is, 'I am the Good Shepherd. I have come to seek and to save the lost. I have come to seek and to save you.'"

The Phantom masked his misshapen face and longed for Christine to "make his song take flight." The man with the withered hand masked the reality of his withered hand and longed for a healing touch. Jesus reached out to the man in the temple that day and invited the man to stretch out his hand. Imagine the shock that registered in this man's consciousness when he contemplated unmasking his hand for all to see. What shame! But he did it, and his hand was made whole. Like that man, we are all invited to unmask our bent-out-of-shape lives to the Savior, Jesus Christ. Jesus says to us through this story, "I know who you are behind all your masks. I know you for what you really are. And I love you just as you are." That's what the Phantom found in Christine, but only for a moment. We find it in Jesus for an eternity. The song is ours to sing to Jesus: "You alone, dear Jesus, can make my song take flight."

The Madonna holds the Crucified One. That's our visual image. It's an image that reminds us of our own deep human sinfulness.

Jesus was crucified for us. If the Madonna could speak, what words of promise might she whisper to us? She might say something like this: "Here is your Christ child. Here is your crucified Savior. He died for my sins. He died for your sins. He died that you might be released from the bondage of sin. Go, therefore, and live a life free of sin's bondage."

Visuals with an Image Sermon

When a sermon is organized around a single image, the use of visuals would match that focus. Consider the example of a sermon focused on Michelangelo's *Pietà* (see page 90). A dramatic way to present this visual image would be to project the image from the very beginning to the end of the sermon. If your congregation lacks the equipment for projecting an image for such a sermon, a relatively low-tech solution would be to download a copy of the image (you can search for it with Google, as described in chapter 4). Print it in your bulletin, and ask people to have it in hand throughout your sermon.

A visual or verbal image functions well as the organizing center of the sermon when you find images that are powerful enough. The *Pietà* is one such example. There are many others. Building an entire sermon around a single image is certainly not the only way to use visual images in preaching. As we've heard from a variety of parish pastors, the possibilities for the use of images in preaching are as diverse as the human imagination.

Conclusion

Thinking in picture is an idea that has stirred controversy and sparked imaginations. In our review of the church's use of picture through much of its history, we've encountered arguments for and against the use of pictures in the church. We've seen the favored status granted to words over images in the Enlightenment world of the West, and I've presented a case for a greater balance between words and images in our communication of the gospel. Chapter 4's summary of the ideas from a number of parish pastors provides valuable advice in the nuts and bolts of thinking in picture. Finally, this chapter offers a variety of sermon structures, along with suggestions for incorporating images (including verbal images) into each.

If you take up this challenge, will it work? Is there any proof that visual images actually communicate the gospel to hungry hearts? I doubt there is any proof of the matter, any more than we have scientific proof that the words we speak in our preaching work. Can the Holy Spirit breathe life upon those who hear our words? I'm convinced that is possible. Can the Holy Spirit breathe life upon those who view our images? I'm convinced that is possible as well. Preach in words and images, poetry and painting, and entrust the effectiveness of your preaching to God's Holy Breath.

The challenge now falls upon you. How shall you appropriate this material? Should you plunge ahead into this thinking-in-picture world? This is a serious question, and no one can answer it for you. Perhaps the best people with whom you should talk this over are the leaders of your own parish. Enlist them in conversation. Look at all the aspects of the matter. Think about the finances involved. Pray for guidance. May our good Lord guide all of us as we think seriously on this matter of great change and seek to fulfill our callings as preachers of the gospel of Jesus Christ.

A biblical passage that guides me in this and in many situations of life and ministry is 1 Corinthians 9:19–23. Paul is giving a defense of his ministry of the gospel. Why does he do what he does? He indicates that he uses a grand variety of strategies in his presentation of the gospel message. "To the Jews I became as a Jew," he writes. "To those under the law I became as one under the law. . . . To those outside the law I became as one outside the law. . . . To the weak I became weak, so that I might win the weak. I have become all things to all people, that I might by all means save some. I do it all for the sake of the gospel, so that I may share in its blessings."

Do it all for the sake of the gospel!

Notes

Introduction: Thinking in Picture

1. Marshall McLuhan, *The Gutenberg Galaxy: The Making of Typographic Man* (Toronto: University of Toronto Press, 1962), 38, 65.

2. Joel W. Martin and Conrad E. Ostwalt Jr., eds., *Screening the Sacred: Religion, Myth, and Ideology in Popular American Film* (San Francisco: Oxford Press, 1995), 153.

3. Robert K. Johnston, *Reel Spirituality: Theology and Film in Dialogue* (Grand Rapids: Baker, 2000), 95.

4. William A. Dyrness, *Visual Faith: Art, Theology, and Worship in Dialogue* (Grand Rapids: Baker, 2001), 20–21.

5. Ibid., 132–33.

6. W. J. T. Mitchell, *Iconology: Image, Text, Ideology* (Chicago: University of Chicago Press, 1986), 9–10.

7. Jeremy Begbie, ed., *Beholding the Glory: Incarnation through the Arts* (Grand Rapids: Baker, 2001), xii–xiii.

8. Dyrness, *Visual Faith*, 11.

9. Ibid., 13–14.

10. Johnston, *Reel Spirituality*, 74–75.

11. Dyrness, *Visual Faith*, 130.

12. Ibid., 21.

1. The Painted Word

1. Margaret Miles, *Image as Insight: Visual Understanding in Western Christianity and Secular Culture* (Boston: Beacon, 1985), 4–5.

2. Neil Macgregor with Erika Langmuir, *Seeing Salvation: Images of Christ in Art* (New Haven: Yale University Press, 2000), 22.

3. Ibid., 23.

4. Jane Dillenberger, *Style and Content in Christian Art* (New York: Crossroad, 1986), 39–40.

5. Ibid., 30.

6. Ibid., 7.

7. Helen De Borchgrave, *A Journey into Christian Art* (Minneapolis: Fortress Press, 2000), 7.

8. Ibid., 7.

9. Jeremy Begbie, *Beholding the Glory: Incarnation through the Arts* (Grand Rapids: Baker, 2001), 86.

10. Janet R. Walton, *Art and Worship: A Vital Connection* (Wilmington, Del.: Glazier, 1988), 25–27.

11. Ibid.

12. William A. Dyrness, *Visual Faith: Art, Theology, and Worship in Dialogue* (Grand Rapids: Baker, 2001), 26–27.

13. Richard Viladesau, *Theology and Art: Encountering God through Music, Art and Rhetoric* (New York: Paulist Press, 2000), 28.

14. Ibid., 25.

15. De Borchgrave, *A Journey into Christian Art*, 7.

16. Miles, *Image as Insight*, 42.

17. Ibid., 45, 51, 53. See also Macgregor with Langmuir, *Seeing Salvation*, 25: "As a consequence, Christian art inevitably moved from a domestic to a monumental scale, a development that quickened after 324, when Christianity became a state religion and grandiose churches began to be commissioned by the emperor himself."

18. Miles, *Image as Insight*, 57.

19. Ibid., 53.

20. De Borchgrave, *A Journey into Christian Art*, 70ff, 93.

21. Dillenberger, *Style and Content in Christian Art*, 58.

22. Ibid., 61.

23. Jaroslav Pelikan, *The Spirit of Eastern Christendom, 2 (600–1700)* (Chicago: University of Chicago Press, 1974), 105.

24. Walton, *Art and Worship*, 40–41.

25. Dillenberger, *Style and Content in Christian Art*, 65.

26. Miles, *Image as Insight*, 65–66.

27. Ibid.

28. Ibid., 67.

29. Carlos M. N. Eire, *War against Idols: The Reformation of Worship from Erasmus to Calvin* (Cambridge: Cambridge University Press, 1986), 1, 11.

30. Dyrness, *Visual Faith*, 51.

31. Miles, *Image as Insight*, 99.

2. Iconoclastic Controversies

1. Jeremy Begbie, ed., *Beholding the Glory: Incarnation through the Arts* (Grand Rapids: Baker, 2001), 89.

2. Lee Palmer Wandel, *Voracious Idols and Violent Hands: Iconoclasm in Reformation Zurich, Strasbourg, and Basel* (New York: Cambridge University Press, 1995), 26.

3. Begbie, *Beholding the Glory*, 88.

4. Jaroslav Pelikan, *Imago Dei: The Byzantine Apologia for Icons* (Princeton: Princeton University Press, 1990), 8.

5. Ibid., 116.

6. John of Damascus, trans. David Anderson, *On the Divine Images: Three Apologies against Those Who Attack the Divine Images* (Crestwood, N.Y.: St. Vladimir's Seminary Press, 1980).

7. Ibid., 8.

8. Ibid., 21.

9. Ibid., 33.

10. Ibid., 25.

11. Ibid., 37.

12. Ibid., 64.

13. Ibid., 47.

14. Ibid., 72.

15. Ibid., 73–74.

16. Jaroslav Pelikan, *The Spirit of Eastern Christendom, 2 (600–1700)* (Chicago: University of Chicago Press, 1974), 91.

17. Pelikan, *Imago Dei*, 67.

18. Pelikan, *The Spirit of Eastern Christendom*, 121–22.

19. Ibid., 131.

20. Neil Macgregor with Erika Langmuir, *Seeing Salvation: Images of Christ in Art* (New Haven: Yale University Press, 2000), 86.

21. Ibid., 13.

22. Pelikan, *Imago Dei*, 77.

23. Ibid., 79.

24. Ibid., 84.

25. Ibid., 99.

26. Begbie, *Beholding the Glory*, 87.

27. Pelikan, *The Spirit of Eastern Christendom*, 129.

28. Ibid., 115.

29. Begbie, *Beholding the Glory*, 96.

30. William A. Dyrness, *Visual Faith: Art, Theology, and Worship in Dialogue* (Grand Rapids: Baker, 2001), 34.

31. Begbie, *Beholding the Glory*, 90.

32. Carl E. Braaten and Robert W. Jenson, eds., *Union with Christ: The New Finnish Interpretation of Luther* (Grand Rapids: Eerdmans, 1998), 25–26.

33. Ibid., 38.

34. Dietrich Bonhoeffer, *Worldly Preaching: Lectures on Homiletics* (New York: Crossroad, 1991), 101.

35. Pelikan, *Imago Dei,* 117.

36. Pelikan, *The Spirit of Eastern Christendom,* 121.

37. Ibid., 133.

38. Margaret Miles, *Image as Insight: Visual Understanding in Western Christianity and Secular Culture* (Boston: Beacon, 1985), 118.

39. Ibid.

40. Carlos M. N. Eire, *War against Idols: The Reformation of Worship from Erasmus to Calvin* (Cambridge: Cambridge University Press, 1986), 2.

41. Ibid., 3.

42. Wandel, *Voracious Idols and Violent Hands,* 3.

43. Eire, *War against Idols,* 28, 31, 33, 34.

44. Ibid., 53.

45. Ibid., 55, 56, 59.

46. Ibid., 59.

47. Ibid., 69.

48. Miles, *Image as Insight,* 99.

49. Wandel, *Voracious Idols and Violent Hands,* 96–97.

50. Miles, *Image as Insight,* 102–103.

51. Eire, *War against Idols,* 84–85.

52. Miles, *Image as Insight,* 104.

53. Dyrness, *Visual Faith,* 54–55.

54. Ibid., 54.

55. Ibid., 52–53.

56. Eire, *War against Idols,* 200.

57. Ibid., 197ff.

58. Ibid.

59. Ibid., 206–208.

60. Ibid.

61. Ibid., 231.

62. Ibid., 232.

63. Martin Luther, "Against the Heavenly Prophets in the Matter of Images and Sacraments," in *Luther's Works,* vol. 40, *Church and Ministry II,* ed. Conrad Bergendorff (Philadelphia: Muhlenberg, 1958), 81–82.

64. Ibid., 89.

65. Ibid., 90–91.

66. Ibid., 88.

67. Ibid., 91.

68. Ibid., 92.

69. Eire, *War against Idols,* 220.

70. Luther, "Against the Heavenly Prophets," 84.

71. Ibid., 99.

72. Ibid., 99–100.

73. Macgregor, *Seeing Salvation,* 202.

74. Eive, *War against Idols,* 216.

75. Paul Althaus, trans. Robert C. Schultz, *The Theology of Martin Luther* (Philadelphia: Fortress Press, 1970), 194, 183.

76. Robert K. Johnston, *Reel Spirituality: Theology and Film in Dialogue* (Grand Rapids: Baker, 2000), 76.

77. Miles, *Image as Insight,* 123.

3. Poetry and Painting

1. W. J. T. Mitchell, *Iconology: Image, Text, Ideology* (Chicago: University of Chicago Press, 1986), 3.

2. Ibid., 49.

3. Ibid., 43.

4. Ibid., 110.

5. Ibid., 113.

6. Ibid.

7. Edwin A. Burtt, *Types of Religious Philosophy* (New York: Harper & Brothers, 1951), 45.

8. Jeremy Begbie, *Beholding the Glory: Incarnation through the Arts* (Grand Rapids: Baker, 2001), 7.

9. Ibid.

10. Ibid., 8.

11. Burtt, *Types of Religious Philosophy,* 56.

12. William A. Dyrness, *Visual Faith: Art, Theology, and Worship in Dialogue* (Grand Rapids: Baker, 2001), 145.

13. Leonard Schlain, *The Alphabet versus the Goddess* (New York: Penguin, 1998), ix.

14. Ibid., p. viii.

15. Ibid., 1.

16. Ibid., 7.

17. Ibid., 39.

18. Margaret Miles, *Image as Insight: Visual Understanding in Western Christianity and Secular Culture* (Boston: Beacon, 1985), 28.

19. Ibid., 36.

20. Ibid., 5.

21. Ibid., 143.

22. Ibid., 144.

23. Ibid.

24 Ibid., 145

25. Ibid.

26. Ibid.

27. Ibid., 150–51.

28. Dyrness, *Visual Faith,* 156.

29. Ibid., 52–53.

30. Helmut T. Lehmann, ed., *Luther's Works,* vol. 6, *Word and Sacrament I,* ed. E. Theodore Bachmann (Philadelphia: Muhlenberg, 1960), 123.

31. Janet R. Walton, *Art and Worship: A Vital Connection* (Wilmington, Del.: Glazier, 1988), 112.

32. Andrey Tarkovsky, *Sculpting in Time: Reflections on the Cinema* (Austin: University of Texas Press, 1986), 36–37, 43, 49. Italics in original.

33. Pierre Babin, *The New Era in Religious Communication* (Minneapolis: Fortress Press, 1991).

34. Robert Wuthnow, *All in Sync: How Music and Art Are Revitalizing American Religion* (Berkeley: University of California Press, 2003), 16, 18. Italics in original.

35. Ibid., 31, 32.

36. Ibid., 75ff.

37. Ibid., 155.

38. Ibid., xiv.

4. Visualizing Salvation

1. Timothy J. Stidham, "Jesus Meets the Matrix: Preaching Holiness in a Digital World," D. Min. thesis for the ACTS D. Min. in Preaching Program, 2002, 9.

2. Ibid., 35–36.

3. Ibid., 38.

5. Sermon Structures

1. See Richard A. Jensen, *Thinking in Story: Preaching in a Post-literate Age* (Lima, Ohio: C.S.S., 1993).

2. For a full discussion of the New Homiletic and the use of story, see Eugene Lowry, *The Sermon: Dancing the Edge of Mystery* (Nashville: Abingdon, 1997). My contributions to the New Homiletic and the use of story in preaching have been set forth in several books, including *Telling the Story: Variety and Imagination in Preaching* (Minneapolis: Augsburg, 1980); and *Thinking in Story.*

3. Eugene L. Lowry, *How to Preach a Parable: Designs for Narrative Sermons* (Nashville: Abingdon, 1989).

4. Robert Alter, *The Art of Biblical Narrative* (New York: Basic, 1983), 7.

5. See Richard A. Jensen, *Preaching Matthew's Gospel: A Narrative Approach* (Lima, Ohio: C.S.S., 1998); *Preaching Mark's Gospel: A Narrative*

Approach (Lima, Ohio: C.S.S., 1996); and *Preaching Luke's Gospel: A Narrative Approach* (Lima, Ohio: C.S.S., 1997).

6. Robert Farrar Capon, *The Fingerprints of God: Tracking the Divine Suspect through a History of Images* (Grand Rapids: Eerdmans, 2000), 14.

7. Ibid., 19.

8. Ibid.

9. Patricia Wilson-Kastner, *Imagery for Preaching* (Minneapolis: Fortress Press, 1989), 19–21.

10. David Schlafer, *Preaching as Image, Story and Idea: Sermons That Work VII* (Harrisburg, Pa.: Morehouse, 1988), 46–48.

11. Ibid.

Bibliography

Althaus, Paul. *The Theology of Martin Luther*. Translated by Robert C. Schultz. Philadelphia: Fortress Press, 1970.

Babin, Pierre. *The New Era in Religious Communication*. Minneapolis: Fortress Press, 1991.

Begbie, Jeremy, ed. *Beholding the Glory: Incarnation through the Arts*. Grand Rapids: Baker, 2001.

Bonhoeffer, Dietrich. *Worldly Preaching: Lectures on Homiletics*. New York: Crossroad, 1991.

Braaten, Carl E., and Robert W. Jenson, eds. *Union with Christ: The New Finnish Interpretation of Luther*. Grand Rapids: Eerdmans, 1998.

Burtt, Edwin A. *Types of Religious Philosophy*. New York: Harper, 1951.

Capon, Robert Farrar. *The Fingerprints of God: Tracking the Divine Suspect through a History of Images*. Grand Rapids: Eerdmans, 2000.

Damascus, John. *On the Divine Images: Three Apologies against Those Who Attack the Divine Images*. Translated by David Anderson. Crestwood, N.Y.: St. Vladimir's Seminary Press, 1980.

DeBorchgrave, Helen. *A Journey into Christian Art*. Minneapolis: Fortress Press, 2000.

Dillenberger, Jane. *Style and Content in Christian Art*. New York: Crossroads, 1986.

Drury, John. *Painting the Word: Christian Pictures and Their Meanings*. New Haven: Yale University Press, 1999.

Dyrness, William A. *Visual Faith: Art, Theology, and Worship in Dialogue*. Grand Rapids: Baker, 2001.

Eire, Carlos M. N. *War against Idols: The Reformation of Worship from Erasmus to Calvin*. Cambridge: Cambridge University Press, 1986.

Jensen, Richard A. *Preaching Luke's Gospel: A Narrative Approach*. Lima, Ohio: C.S.S., 1997.

————. *Preaching Mark's Gospel: A Narrative Approach.* Lima, Ohio: C.S.S., 1996.

————. *Preaching Matthew's Gospel: A Narrative Approach.* Lima, Ohio: C.S.S., 1998.

————. *Telling the Story: Variety and Imagination in Preaching.* Minneapolis: Augsburg, 1980.

————. *Thinking in Story: Preaching in a Post-literate Age.* Lima, Ohio: C.S.S., 1993.

Johnston, Robert K. *Reel Spirituality: Theology and Film in Dialogue.* Grand Rapids: Baker Academic, 2001.

Lehman, Helmut T., and E. Theodore Bachmann, eds. *Luther's Works,* 54 vols., vol. 6, *Word and Sacrament I.* Philadelphia: Muhlenberg, 1960.

Lowry, Eugene. *How to Preach a Parable: Designs for Narrative Sermons.* Nashville: Abingdon, 1989.

————. *The Sermon: Dancing on the Edge of Mystery.* Nashville: Abingdon, 1999.

Luther, Martin. "Against the Heavenly Prophets in the Matter of Images and Sacraments." In *Luther's Works,* vol. 40, *Church and Ministry I,* edited by Conrad Bergendorff. Philadelphia: Muhlenberg, 1958.

Macgregor, Neil, with Erika Langmuir. *Seeing Salvation: Images of Christ in Art.* New Haven: Yale University Press, 2000.

Martin, Joel W., and Conrad E. Ostwalt Jr., eds. *Screening the Sacred: Religion, Myth, and Ideology in Popular American Film.* San Francisco: Oxford, 1995.

McLuhan, Marshall. *The Gutenberg Galaxy: The Making of Typographic Man.* Toronto: University of Toronto Press, 1962.

Miles, Margaret. *Image as Insight: Visual Understanding in Western Christianity and Secular Culture.* Boston: Beacon, 1985.

Mitchell, W. J. T. *Iconology: Image, Text, Ideology.* Chicago: University of Chicago Press, 1986.

Pelikan, Jaroslav. *Imago Dei: The Byzantine Apologia for Icons.* Princeton: Princeton University Press, 1990.

————. *The Spirit of Eastern Christendom, 2 (600–1700).* Chicago: University of Chicago Press, 1974.

Schlafer, David. *Preaching as Image, Story and Idea: Sermons That Work VII.* Harrisburg, Pa.: Morehouse, 1988.

Schlain, Leonard. *The Alphabet versus the Goddess.* New York: Penguin, 1998.

Stidham, Timothy J. "Jesus Meets the Matrix: Preaching Holiness in a Digital World," D. Min. thesis, ACTS D. Min. in Preaching Program, 2002.

Stone, Karen. *Image and Spirit: Finding Meaning in Visual Art.* Minneapolis: Augsburg, 2003.

Tarkovsky, Andrey. *Sculpting in Time: Reflections on the Cinema.* Austin: University of Texas Press, 1986.

Viladesau, Richard. *Theology and Art: Encountering God through Music, Art and Rhetoric.* New York: Paulist, 2000.

Walton, Janet, R. *Art and Worship: A Vital Connection.* Wilmington, Del.: Glazier, 1988.

Wandel, Lee Palmer. *Voracious Idols and Violent Hands: Iconoclasm in Reformation Zurich, Strasbourg, and Basel.* New York: Cambridge University Press, 1995.

Williams, Rowan. *The Indwelling of the Light: Praying with Icons of Christ.* Grand Rapids: Eerdmans, 2003.

Wilson-Kastner, Patricia. *Imagery for Preaching.* Minneapolis: Fortress Press, 1989.

Wuthnow, Robert. *All in Sync: How Music and Art Are Revitalizing American Religion.* Berkeley: University of California Press, 2003.

Index

About the CD-ROM

The CD-ROM includes a PowerPoint document containing the following:

• A summary of each chapter in Richard A. Jensen's book, *Envisioning the Word: The Use of Visual Images in Preaching.*

• A number of Internet links throughout for you to click on and explore on the Web.

• A wealth of original sacred image icons—use these to jumpstart your thinking about using visuals in sermons. Owners of *Envisioning the Word* have permission to use the black-and-white icon images as needed in liturgies and sermons.

• A searchable PDF of the entire text of *Envisioning the Word.*

Minimum System Requirements

• Microsoft PowerPoint or compatible software

• Adobe Reader (free installer available on CD-ROM)